ULTIMATE SUPERSTARS

SELENA GOMEZ

For Tim

CONTENTS

CHAPTER 1

CHANGING THE GAME

"I'm telling you to trust yourselves – always."

Selena Gomez crossed the stage to touch the hands of her fans in the front row. As she did, hundreds of hands reached up to grab hers. Tucked under her right arm was a piece of paper, her speech. But she didn't use it. She didn't need to. Selena knew exactly what she wanted to say to her audience at WE Day, California.

She told them that she had always dreamed of being an actress, but how, aged eleven, a casting director had told her she wasn't good enough.

"I'm sure all of you have been told that you're not good enough. It crushes you. And it almost did for me..."

It hardly seemed possible. Selena Gomez – the singing star and actor, with over 100 million followers on social media – *not good enough*? Surely everyone had always told her how amazing she was?

"But there was my mom, next to me," explained Selena, "and she said that the most important thing was to always *trust in myself*. She told me to keep going. If I didn't believe I could do it, I wouldn't be here."

The fans were silent as the charismatic young woman onstage told them about her mother – how she had believed in her and worked four jobs, sacrificing everything for Selena's success. It was inspiring to hear Selena's story, to know that she had struggled.

"I live a very blessed life," Selena told her fans. "I have so much to be thankful for, and you are such a big part of inspiring me. You inspire me to be better. We should all inspire each other to be better."

The WE Day audience erupted into cheers. This was why they were here: these thousands of teens wanted to make the world a better place. WE Day was a global movement, all about taking action. It wasn't just grown-ups who could change the world! The kids in the audience had amazing ideas for making their communities, their cities, and even the world, better places. Seeing Selena onstage and hearing her powerful message had given them the strength to believe in themselves and what they could achieve.

Selena went on to explain about the pressure of fame: being told to look a certain way, behave a certain way... "I'm sure you can all relate. You all have pressure that you have to deal with every day."

Selena paused. Her expression was serious.

"Until recently, I had given in to that pressure. I lost sight of who I was. I tried to change who I am because I thought that others would accept me for it."

Now her voice cracked. Looking out at the sea of faces in front of her, Selena was on the verge of tears.

"And I realised that I don't know how to be anything but myself..."

Fans were hugging each other, crying, holding

the hands of the friends next to them. *Be yourself. Don't let anybody change you.* It was the message they wanted to hear. Their heroine was speaking to them like a friend, sharing her doubts and her anxieties.

"Please just be kind to each other," Selena continued. "Please stay true to yourself. Please just remain who you are and know that we have each other's backs. I've learned from my mistakes. I want you to know that I know what it's like. You are who you surround yourself with. I hope I can inspire you to trust yourself to love and to be loved."

"Let's change the game," Selena said. "This is such a beautiful thing that you're doing. Be proud of yourselves."

CHAPTER 2

GRAND PRAIRIE

When Mandy Cornett realised she was pregnant, she was only fifteen.

Teen pregnancy wasn't unusual in Grand Prairie – but Mandy was dismayed. She had ambition. She wanted to be an actor when she left school. Having a baby in her teens? This was not the future she had imagined for herself.

Mandy put on a brave face, but really she wished she could run away. She had never been popular at school. The other kids bullied her for her purple hair and her combat boots. She didn't like the same music or films or fashion as them. Mandy had always been different. And now there was another, *big* reason to pick on her...

Of course, everyone guessed instantly who the father of Mandy's baby was: Ricardo Gomez, or "Ricky" as everyone called him.

Ricky was sixteen, a year older than Mandy. Would they stay together? Would they get married? Everyone around the couple had questions. It felt like a soap opera – but not one Mandy and Ricky wanted to be in.

So they went to their parents for advice. Both Mandy's and Ricky's parents were happily married. They gave the only answer they could. Mandy and Ricky must do what their hearts told them to.

Eventually the teenagers came to a decision: they would get married. Once their baby was born, they would go back to high school to get the qualifications they needed to find jobs. They knew it wouldn't be easy, but they loved each other.

Feeling nervous, scared and excited, Mandy and Ricky waited as the months went by and their new life got closer and closer.

Finally, on 22 July, 1992, Selena Marie Gomez was born.

Baby Selena was the most beautiful thing her parents had ever seen. Her father's family was Mexican and she had inherited their dark hair and long lashes. She had her mother's deep, brown eyes.

When she picked up her tiny child, Mandy's heart felt like it was going to explode. Lying in a hospital bed, with her own parents sitting beside her, she didn't know whether to laugh or cry; she felt like a child and an adult both at once. But every time she held her newborn baby in her arms, all the confusion was swept away by a flood of love.

Lots of couples argue about baby names, but Mandy and Ricky agreed easily... twice. Priscilla had been their first choice, but Selena's cousin Priscilla had been born just six months earlier. Instead they named their child after Selena Quintanilla, one of their favourite singers, who had also been born in Texas.

At the time of Selena's birth, Mandy was sixteen and Ricky seventeen. It was agreed that Ricky's parents, Ricardo and Mary, and Mandy's parents, Debbie and David, would look after the baby while the teenagers went back to school.

So, from eight thirty in the morning till four in the afternoon, the new parents pretended to be normal teenagers again. The responsibility of having a baby had changed them, though – Mandy especially. She had never tried very hard in school. She hadn't seen the point of studying. Now, however, she started working... *hard*. Mandy wanted to make a success of her life – not just for herself but for baby Selena.

Over the months that followed, Mandy soared from the bottom of the class right to the top. By the time final exams came round, she came first in her class. She was also voted prom queen.

The girl with the purple hair suddenly seemed to have things sorted. Everything had changed for Mandy.

Finally, now that school was over, Mandy and Ricky could be a family at last. Baby Selena was the apple of her parents' eye. Selena's grandparents adored her too, and they continued to help with childcare so that Mandy and Ricky could work.

Cherished by all, Selena was growing fast: from a happy, healthy baby to a bouncing, energetic toddler, then a confident preschooler. Young Selena knew just how to get what she wanted – she might be small, but she was bold and full of character! And the way she imitated grownup behaviour made her parents howl with laughter. What would their little Selena be like as a teenager? At three and a half, she was already acting the part!

But life for Selena's parents was hard. As high-school graduates with little experience, they could expect only low wages for long hours. Every penny they earned was spent on food, rent, and fuel to run their car. There were no luxuries in the Gomez household – and with the pressure of having to support a family, Mandy's dream of being an actress seemed to be slipping away. She found herself waiting on tables and sweeping floors instead.

Selena's parents tried not to argue during the tough times, but it was difficult. There always seemed to be problems. Their fridge was broken. The car wouldn't start. There was a leak in the roof...

Mandy and Ricky started to blame each other for every small thing that went wrong. The one ray of sunshine? Bright, bubbly, playful Selena. She kept them smiling, no matter what. Her laughter and her big, beautiful grin were infectious.

But by the time Selena turned five, Ricky and Mandy had become so unhappy in their marriage that they began to question whether they should stay together. They were worried the tension in the house wasn't good for Selena either.

"We can't go on like this," Mandy told Ricky. "It's not working."

Ricky nodded. "We need to get a divorce."

It was the first time in months that the couple had agreed on anything.

"We've done the best we could," Mandy sighed. They looked at each other – both were thinking the same thing. Telling their daughter would be the hardest thing in the world.

They were right. Five-year-old Selena's eyes were wide with horror as her parents explained that they had decided to split up.

"But you can't! We're a family," she cried.

"We'll be happier if we live apart, *mija*," explained Ricky.

"What about me? I want to live with both of you!"

"We love you very much," Mandy told her. "Nothing will change that – ever. You'll just have two homes instead of one."

But little Selena knew that everything would change. On the TV programmes she watched, when parents divorced, mums got new boyfriends and dads got new girlfriends. And the new partners were always horrible to their new stepchildren. Always.

"I hate you! Both of you!" Selena stomped out of the room, slamming the door behind her.

"Selena! Come back!"

But Selena refused.

Over the next few weeks, she wouldn't listen to anything her parents said to reassure her. The only people she could talk to were her grandparents.

"You're scared right now, but it's going to be OK, honey," Nana Debbie told her. "Your mom and your dad will always be there for you – and so will we."

"We sure will." Grandpa David smiled.

Debbie and David felt like second parents to Selena. She had spent so much time with them when she was little. If they said it was going to be OK, maybe it would.

But she couldn't get rid of the nugget of worry in her chest – and she couldn't help blaming her parents for breaking up their family. It would take a long time to change that.

Time passed, and like Nana had said, the important things *did* stay the same. Selena still spent time with both her parents. She lived with Mandy, and Ricky came to take her out at weekends. Slowly, as she got used to it, not being together as a family felt a little less painful.

Money was still a problem though. As Selena got older, Mandy wanted her to have what other girls had: clothes, trips to theme parks and museums, CDs, concerts... She could see her daughter loved music with a passion.

At times, Mandy had to work four jobs just to pay the rent. Sometimes the car ran out of fuel on the way to school. There was no money for holidays or other luxuries – and Mandy hated to ask Debbie and David for help.

Alongside her other jobs, Selena's mum was still trying to find work as an actress. She was determined not to give up on her dream. Grand Prairie was too small to offer many opportunities, so when the right roles came along, Mandy travelled across Texas, taking Selena with her. Bringing Selena to the theatre was cheaper than hiring a childminder!

Although Mandy brought along books and toys for Selena to play with, her daughter's attention was always on the stage. Selena loved to watch her mum act – and she had strong opinions too...

"You know, Mom, it might be funnier if you did it differently," she said one day, after watching Mandy rehearse a comedy.

Her mother smiled. Selena's favourite game was putting on productions with her friends. She always took the role of director, telling the others where to stand and how to say their lines. "How do you think I should do it then?" she asked her daughter.

Little Selena's face was serious. "It would be

better if you pause for longer before you say the last word. And you could put your hands on your hips or something. Maybe roll your eyes? That would be funny."

Wow, those suggestions weren't bad at all. Mandy's six-year-old daughter had an amazing grasp of what would work onstage and what wouldn't!

And Selena's talent didn't just lie in directing others. She could play any character: witches, princesses, pirates... Her favourite roles were the funny ones, and she could imitate anyone. Selena's impersonations of the actors who performed alongside Mandy were hilarious – and sometimes painfully accurate!

"She's going to be an actress, I'm sure of it," Mandy told Debbie. "She's far more confident than I was at her age."

"She's got a special talent," Selena's nana agreed. "Look at those shows that she puts on. All those voices, all those different roles... She's amazing."

It was true. Singing, dancing, acting – whenever she had an audience, Selena shone.

But, Mandy wondered, would there be enough

opportunities here in Grand Prairie for a budding young actress?

CHAPTER 3

BIG BREAK

"Listen to this, Selena. There's going to be a casting call for *Barney and Friends*! Next weekend!"

Mandy was flushed with excitement. She had spotted a notice for the casting on the bulletin board at the theatre where she was working and had hurried home as fast as she could to tell her daughter. Barney was one of the most popular children's shows on TV. Why wasn't Selena more excited?

"*Barney's* for babies, Mom!"

Selena was nine. She was in third grade. She *certainly* didn't watch *Barney and Friends* any more!

"Sweetheart, the children who *perform* on the show aren't babies. They're lots of different ages."

Selena frowned. "Really?"

"Yes! I think you should audition. You'd get to act... *and* sing."

Mandy knew this would get Selena interested. Her daughter loved singing. She had a lovely voice – sweet and clear, mature for her age. Selena's hero was Britney Spears. She performed Britney's songs and dance routines over and over again.

"You'll make new friends too," added Mandy.

Selena put on her thinking face. *Barney* was definitely for babies... but it would be proper acting. "I want to do it," she said finally.

Mandy gave her a hug. "That's great, honey. Maybe we should watch a few episodes of *Barney* to prepare for the audition?"

"Sure." Selena grimaced comically.

But, secretly, Selena still loved the big purple dinosaur and his friends. The show reminded her of being little, watching it at her grandparents' house.

"Can I have a cookie and some milk while we're watching?"

Her mum laughed. "Did someone just say they *weren't* a baby?!"

The audition for *Barney and Friends* was on a Saturday afternoon.

By now, Mandy had brought her daughter to several TV and theatre castings, so Selena knew just what to do. First of all, she queued up at the desk to write down her name and address. Wow – there were hundreds of names already on the list!

Selena looked nervously around the room. It was packed with children and their parents. Despite what her mum had said, she was one of the oldest.

"Those kids are still in diapers," she whispered.

"They're not!" said Mandy. "They must be at least five."

Selena frowned. "How do they learn their lines if they're only five?" she wondered.

The girl who was behind them in the line seemed to be about her age though. Selena glanced up at her mum, who gave a nod of encouragement. Selena smiled. "Hi, I'm Selena Gomez. What's your name?"

"I'm Demi Lovato," the girl replied, with a confident smile. "I'm from Dallas."

"I'm from Grand Prairie," said Selena.

There was a pause, then the two girls asked at the same time: "Who's your favourite singer?"

They both giggled. In an instant, Selena and Demi forgot about the audition and began to get to know one another.

Both girls loved Britney Spears. Demi was learning the piano. Selena wanted to be an actress and singer when she grew up. Selena sometimes did beauty pageants. Their birthdays were just one month apart. They had so much in common!

"Do you want to do some colouring?" asked Demi, once they'd told each other everything they could think of. She pulled a book from her rucksack. "Here, we can sit on my coat."

But then...

"Selena Gomez!" called the casting director's assistant. "Come through, please."

"It's time," said her mum.

"Good luck!" whispered Demi.

"You too," said Selena, and squeezed the hand of her new best friend.

How amazing it would be if she and Demi both got parts on the show!

A month went by, and Selena had almost forgotten about the casting. It was 22 July, and today she had more exciting things to think about. It was her birthday!

She was turning 10. Her grandparents, Debbie and David, had organised a party for all the family. Ricky would be there, and so would her cousin Priscilla. Selena was fizzing with excitement.

Out in the garden, coloured decorations were fluttering in the trees and a table was set with all Selena's favourite treats. Everyone had brought a present, and Selena had squealed with delight as she opened each one. She and her mum didn't have many luxuries, but today she felt like a princess.

Best of all, her nana had baked a huge cake covered in white and pink icing. Her family gathered around to sing 'Happy Birthday', but just as Selena was about to cut the cake, her mum stopped her.

"There's one final gift for you, Selena."

Mandy handed her a thick envelope. It was addressed to *Selena Marie Gomez*, and it looked official. A little shiver of nervousness went up Selena's spine. The whole family was watching her.

Did they know what was inside?

She tore open the envelope, pulled out the sheaf of paper inside and began to read:

Dear Selena Gomez,

Following your recent audition for a role on Barney and Friends, we are delighted to offer you the role of Gianna...

Selena stopped reading and stared around at her family. Her eyes were wide with surprise.

"I've got a part! On *Barney*!"

Mandy, Ricky and the rest of the family burst into whoops of delight. Loudest of all was her cousin, Priscilla, who knew how much Selena wanted to become an actor.

"Wow, Selena. That's amazing!"

Selena was stunned. "How did you know?" she asked her mum. "How did you know it was a 'yes' and not a 'no'?"

Mandy smiled. "The letter came this morning. I knew you'd got a part because the envelope was so thick. It meant there was a contract inside!"

And there was. Selena was holding her first ever contract in her hand. It was official; she was an actor! This must be the best birthday gift anyone had ever had!

There was just one other thing that would make it completely and utterly perfect...

CHAPTER 4

BARNEY

"You got a part too!"

Selena and Demi grabbed each other by the hand and jumped up and down. It was the first day of rehearsals, and their excitement was already off the charts. They were going to be on the show together!

"What's your character called?" asked Selena.

"Angela! And yours?"

"Gianna! Mom says it's Italian."

Selena and Demi quickly became inseparable. Every moment they weren't in front of the camera, they were sharing stories and jokes, discussing their favourite music and giggling about boys.

The girls were together in front of the camera

a lot too. Along with the rest of the cast, they joined Barney the Dinosaur to sing songs and play games, showing young viewers how to use their imagination, work together and talk about their feelings.

There was so much to learn. First, there were lines to remember and actions to get right. Then they had to learn where to stand for each bit of the episode. That was called "blocking". With a giant dinosaur and a big gaggle of children in each scene, sometimes it was hard to get right.

"Gianna!" called the director. "You're masking Angela. Move slightly to your left, please..."

"Masking" meant standing in front of someone. It happened all the time in the first few weeks, while they were learning to spot where the cameras were.

"*Gianna!*"

Demi tapped Selena on the shoulder. "He's talking to you," she whispered.

"Oh! Sorry!" Selena hadn't got used to being called by her character name on set.

"And don't look straight at the camera. Just

notice where it is and make sure your face is always visible."

It was hard at first – there were so many things to think about. But soon it became second nature to the girls: where to look, when to move and how to say their lines. Running around an artificial plastic garden with a huge purple dinosaur had started to feel... completely natural!

But there was a problem. Back at school, Selena and Demi were being bullied for appearing in a kids' show. A show for babies.

"I hate it," Demi told Selena after one particularly bad week. "I don't want to go to school any more."

"Maybe the bullies are just jealous," said Selena.

"I don't care. I want to be homeschooled," Demi told her. "I've asked my mom."

It might have been true that the other kids were jealous – but that didn't stop the insults from hurting. Like her friend, Selena dreaded going to school. It didn't seem fair that a friendly purple dinosaur was making her life so difficult.

Something else was causing Selena anxiety too. Ever since her parents had split up, she had been scared of them getting new partners – a new boyfriend for Mandy or a new girlfriend for Ricky. In books and on TV, stepmums and stepdads were always horrible. Look at Cinderella! Selena knew she had to make sure Mandy and Ricky didn't make bad choices. What if they were blinded by love, like Cinderella's father?

So Selena watched carefully. She even made up a series of tests to check if the new boyfriend or girlfriend was good enough. Eventually, though, Mandy met someone who passed her own tests – *and* Selena's!

His name was Brian Teefey. He was fun, kind, and Selena could see how happy he made her mum. It wasn't easy to accept a new member of their family at first. But as the months went by, Selena found she was able to welcome Brian into their lives. Ricky would always be her dad – but Brian had a special place in her life too.

Selena starred on *Barney* for two years. She had made lots of friends on the show, but now, one by one, they were leaving. Finally, it was Selena and

Demi's turn. At twelve, they were getting too old to be in a show for preschoolers. Selena was sad to say goodbye to the friendly purple dinosaur – but it was true, she was far too old for clapping games and singing songs about numbers!

"What do I do now, Mom?" Selena asked Mandy, when they got home after the last day of filming. She had an empty feeling inside. She didn't like the thought of just going to school every day. She knew how much she would miss her *Barney* friends and being at the studio.

Mandy hugged her. She hated to see her daughter looking sad.

"We'll go to some auditions," she told Selena. "You're 12. There's so much you can do now."

And it wasn't long before the perfect audition came along.

CHAPTER 5

DISNEY CHANNEL

"Let's go ahead and do the goat scene," the casting director told Selena. "You can start when you're ready."

To anyone else, it would have sounded weird, but Selena was more than ready for "the goat scene". In fact, she had been practising it for weeks. The character she was playing had helped to steal a goat and now wanted to return it. Selena didn't have the rest of the script, so she didn't know why – or what was going to happen!

Selena held the script in her hand, but she didn't need to look at it. She knew the words off by heart. Instead she focused on her expression. In front of her was a camera; she was being filmed for the team of directors and producers to watch later.

"You stole the goat?" Selena made her eyes wide with disbelief.

The casting director read the lines that weren't Selena's. Immediately the scene began to flow. Every time she spoke, Selena managed to sound more and more frustrated. She was determined to get the goat back where it belonged!

"Good," said the casting director. "Do it one more time."

The second time was even better. Selena put more humour into her lines. Confusion. Exasperation. Comical despair.

"You did a great job," said the casting director. "So what do you like to do in your free time, Selena, when you're not acting?"

That was easy. "I love hanging out with my friends," said Selena. "And going to the mall with my mom."

"Do you sing too?"

Selena nodded. She explained that her dream was to become a singer when she was older, like her idol Britney Spears. She wanted to act first, and sing later. She had it all mapped out in her head!

"And do you have any favourite television shows?" asked the casting director.

Selena beamed. She named her favourite shows: *Lizzie McGuire, That's So Raven...*

The casting director smiled. "So you like the Disney Channel?"

Selena nodded. It was true – happily. Because Selena's audition was for none other than Disney!

"I was sitting out there listening to you and your friends," the casting director added, gesturing towards the room outside where Demi and some of Selena's other friends from *Barney* were sitting, waiting for their own auditions. "You're so funny."

Selena beamed with pleasure. Anything to do with her friends always made her smile!

The audition was over. Back in the waiting area, Mandy flung her arms around her daughter, squeezing her tight. "How did it go, honey?"

Selena smiled. "The casting director was really nice. She asked me about how I got into acting, and about singing and stuff. It went OK, I think."

Mandy smiled. At just 12, her daughter never got carried away. Speaking to her was like talking to an adult – especially on the subject of acting. But Mandy knew that underneath her cool exterior, there was nothing Selena wanted more than to be on the Disney Channel.

It wasn't long before there was good news. Selena had been offered her first film role! A small part in an adventure comedy called *Spy Kids*.

Everything on *Spy Kids* was much bigger than on *Barney*. There were more cameras, more production crew, more actors. Selena was also filming on location for the first time. The hair, make-up and costume departments each had a trailer. It was so different and exciting!

Filming took just a day, and as soon as it was over, Selena longed for her next role. The months went by. Finally she was offered a small part in a film called *Walker, Texas Ranger*, also filmed on location.

Then, once again, Selena waited. Fresh auditions came and went. Silence. "Be patient," Mandy told her. But all Selena wanted was to be on set again!

At last Selena received the call she had been waiting for: the Disney Channel wanted her! They invited her to guest star in a teen sitcom, *The Suite Life of Zack & Cody*.

Wow! *Suite Life* was the show everyone was talking about. Forget *Barney*... No one would make fun of her for being on *Suite Life!* The producers had also noticed Selena's beautiful singing voice, and they asked her to record one of the soundtrack songs for the show. Her first ever recording!

There was another first too...

In *Suite Life*, Selena played Cody's girlfriend, Gwen, who is cast to play alongside his best friend Zack in a school performance of *A Midsummer Night's Dream*. While acting a scene, Gwen and Zack fall for each other, to the horror of Zack's girlfriend, Vanessa. The script was so funny and full of twists and turns. Selena loved it, but...

"Eww! Gwen and Zack have to kiss?!"

Selena had never kissed anyone before – on or off set.

She rang Demi.

"What if I can't do it?" she blurted.

"You're an actor," said Demi. "Of course you can."

"But it's not just a quick kiss," wailed Selena. "It's, like, a minute long!"

"You'll be fine," laughed Demi. "It might even be fun!"

Demi was right... sort of. It wasn't fun, but it was fine. It felt weird to think that, months later, thousands of viewers would watch her first on-screen kiss!

A year on, in 2006, fourteen-year-old Selena was cast in her biggest role yet: Mikayla Skeech, Hannah Montana's singing-star rival. *Hannah Montana* was the most popular show on the Disney Channel – this was a big step.

Miley Cyrus, playing Hannah, was already a huge star – and she and Selena became instant friends. Plus, it was fun to play a baddie – Mikayla was so evil!

Selena only starred in two episodes, however. As soon as filming finished, she had that same empty feeling. The big role she wanted still hadn't come along.

One casting director was blunt with her. "You

just don't have what it takes for a lead role."

It was hard to hear. *But maybe it's true*, thought Selena.

At just 14, she knew how lucky she was to being doing something she loved. But perhaps she wasn't good enough for a career as an actor. Maybe she simply didn't have what Miley Cyrus did. Maybe she wasn't cut out to be a star.

Mandy was firm, though. "If you believe you can do it, that's all that matters. Trust yourself. Let the critics be critics, and just *listen to yourself*. Don't give up, Selena."

So with her mum's words in her heart, Selena kept going.

CHAPTER 6

WIZARDS IN NEW YORK

There was someone new in Selena's life, and her name was Alex Russo.

Alex lived in New York with her family, who ran a sandwich shop called Waverly Place. She had two brothers, one older and one younger. She was cool, funny, confident, sometimes sarcastic, and she always knew just how to get what she wanted... especially from her dad, Jerry. She loved her friends and would do anything for her family.

And there was a twist... Alex's family were wizards.

Alex Russo was the lead character on a new show called *Wizards of Waverly Place*. It was due to start in 2007 on the Disney Channel. Selena loved the sound of it: she adored family comedies. Sitting waiting for her audition, she blocked from her mind the words of the casting director who had told her she couldn't play a lead role. She could. She *knew* it.

Selena's audition for *Wizards* was the best she had ever done. Something about the role clicked. Selena was right for Alex, and Alex was right for Selena.

The call from the casting director came almost immediately. The part was Selena's!

Winning the role of Alex Russo was the most incredible thing that had happened to Selena. Finally, she was the lead! But as well as a bubbling feeling of excitement, Selena was also full of nerves. She and Mandy would have to move to LA for filming. Vast, crowded, fast-paced... it would be so different from small Grand Prairie. Would she fit in? Would she make friends? Would her friends from Grand Prairie still keep in touch, from so far away?

But it was like Mandy always told her... trust in herself and everything would be OK.

From the very first day of rehearsals, Selena knew she was going to enjoy playing Alex Russo. She loved the character, and hanging out with the other young actors was so much fun. David Henrie and Jake T. Austin played Selena's on-screen brothers, Justin and Max. As an only child, it was fun to suddenly have two siblings. Selena, David and Jake spent so much time together that they soon began to feel like a family for real.

Selena also fell in love with the bright, friendly set where the show was filmed. There was the "loft" where the Russo family lived, with the New York skyline painted onto the windows. There was the sandwich shop, where Alex and her brothers helped their parents, waiting on tables and washing up. Then there were the street scenes, decorated to look like Greenwich Village, with red-brick buildings, ivy trailing from window boxes and brightly coloured street art... And, finally, there was the wizard lair, the secret room full of potions and magic instruments, where Alex and her brothers learned magic from their dad – and which was also their portal to the wizard world.

The world behind the scenes was equally magical. In the wardrobe department there was rail after rail of clothing for each of the characters – casual clothes, party outfits, fancy dress... Alex had far more clothing than Selena did! The hair and make-up departments were fascinating too. The team spent hours painstakingly transforming actors into all kinds of creatures, such as werewolves, ghouls and monsters.

Not all the action could be filmed on the set itself. Sometimes, Selena and the other cast members acted in front of the "green screen". Later, the images would be superimposed onto other background visuals, for example, the New York skyline.

In the very first episode, Selena's character had to learn to steer a flying carpet over the roofs of the city. At least that's how it appeared on TV! In reality, Selena perched perilously on a carpet draped over some large boxes. The rickety contraption felt just as unstable as a flying carpet! Selena and her on-screen dad, David DeLuise, tumbled off it again and again as they pretended to steer around corners, avoiding skyscrapers.

MELANIE HAMM

"Call it father–daughter bonding," laughed DeLuise as they crashed to the floor – again.
Selena's on-screen mother – Theresa, a mortal – was played by Maria Canals-Barrera, a Latina actress. Selena had never thought that much about her own South American roots. Two of her grandparents – her dad's mum and dad – were Mexican, but her family wasn't very traditional.

Then, one day, a mother ran up to her in the street, waving to catch her attention.

"My kids love you," she told Selena. "We're Mexican and it's so important for them, seeing someone who's like them on TV. Thank you!"

"But I haven't done anything," said Selena, surprised. "I'm just on a kids' show."

"You're a role model! Watching you, Latino kids can believe in their dreams."

Selena felt a glow of pride. She loved the idea that she was inspiring young children. Her own childhood had been tough; she knew how hard it was to keep on believing in yourself. If she could help others, that was better than any magic that Alex could cast with her wizard's wand!

The plot of *Wizards* followed the three Russo children – Alex, Justin and Max – as they competed to become the Family Wizard, taking after their father, Jerry. Only one person in a magical family could be the keeper of the family's powers.

The audience loved the characters – and the popularity of the show quickly grew. Soon, new actors joined. Jennifer Stone was cast as Alex's best friend, Harper Finkle, and eventually Alex also got a boyfriend too: Mason Greenback, who was charming, artistic, British... and a werewolf.

Alex soon found that dating a werewolf wasn't easy. Mason did his best to suppress his werewolf side, but there was only one thing that would allow the couple to be together for ever: Alex needed to win the competition to become the Family Wizard, making her immortal. The fans waited and hoped!

On-screen, the stakes were high – and the same was true off-screen. As *Wizards* got bigger and bigger, Selena's fame was growing too. It felt amazing that so many people loved her show and wanted to know more about her. But sometimes it felt overwhelming. Social media was growing, and it was so easy to share gossip, true or untrue.

Selena tried to simply be herself, but it was impossible to relax. She worried about what the media would say, and she worried about what her fans would think. Would they like her new haircut? Could she go out for dinner without being photographed? Could she trust new people she met? Nothing in her life, big or small, was private any more – and it kind of sucked.

CHAPTER 7

TAYLOR

There was a group of hardworking people surrounding Selena, all of whom were dedicated to making her career a success. Among them were her publicist, her personal assistant, and her managers: her mum, Mandy, and stepdad, Brian. Words couldn't describe how proud Mandy was of her 16-year-old daughter. Every day she was amazed by what talented, warm-hearted Selena had achieved. And the most incredible thing? Selena had only just started. Mandy knew how much more she still had to offer.

Managing Selena's busy TV career didn't leave Mandy much time to relax. But this afternoon, a precious hour had opened up between meetings.

Selena was at the studio rehearsing, and so Mandy made a beeline for one of her favourite places, the Barnes and Noble bookstore. She loved to read, and the tables piled high with bestsellers were so inviting. She began to browse. It was so calm inside the store, unlike the hot, bustling streets of LA.

Mandy wandered into the historical fiction section, then into romance, then fantasy. A display of thrillers caught her eye and, in particular, a striking cover showing a girl sitting on a swing. She picked up a copy. *13 Reasons Why*. It was a book for young adults.

Mandy read the blurb and a shiver went down her spine. She paid for her copy, and began to read it in the cab on the way to her next meeting.

Once she had started, Mandy couldn't put the book down. And an idea came into her head...

"Honey, I want you to read this," she said to Selena that evening, handing her the book. "I think we should meet with the writer."

"Why, Mom?" asked Selena.

"You're going to grow out of Disney one day. I want you to have some amazing projects lined up for when that time comes."

"And you think this book would make good TV?"

"TV or a film," said Mandy. "You'd be great for the lead. If we bought the rights, we could have creative control. Our own show!"

Selena loved the idea – and she loved the book too. Life after Disney seemed so far off, but Mandy was right: one day she would be too old for the world of *Wizards*.

"Let's meet the author," she agreed.

Who knew what the future would hold. But if it involved projects as exciting as this one, Selena couldn't wait.

In the meantime, though, Selena the Disney star was busier than ever. In the weeks when she wasn't filming *Wizards*, Mandy had lined up commercials, interviews, and even her first music video. The song was 'Burnin' Up' by the Jonas Brothers – Joe, Nick and Kevin. Selena's role? Nick's glamorous love interest. It was a small part, but the shoot would change her life.

Nick Jonas had just ended a relationship with *Hannah Montana* star Miley Cyrus. He was blown away by funny, confident, talented Selena. Selena felt the same. She hadn't dated anyone seriously before. Nick was her first celebrity boyfriend, a rising star who would become a major name in a couple of years, after recording the super catchy 'Introducing Me'.

But it wasn't Nick who changed Selena's life.

It was Taylor Swift.

Taylor was also on the shoot, playing Joe's love interest. The two girls clicked instantly. Both were warm, open and generous. They shared the same sense of humour. Taylor understood the pressures of fame – but also saw the funny side of life in the limelight. Selena felt she could tell Taylor anything. She knew her secrets would be safe.

And Taylor was dating Nick's brother, Joe. "Double dates!" squealed Selena. "Can we?"

But when Nick insisted on walking 10 metres ahead of her on a double date in Central Park, New York, Selena began to think twice about her new boyfriend. She liked to be open with her fans. She and Nick were a couple. So what if the public saw them together?

Taylor hung back to walk with her friend.

"What's wrong with Nick?" whispered Selena. "Is he embarrassed for us to be seen together?"

Taylor squeezed her friend's arm. "If he can't handle it, that's his problem."

"We're together. Why can't we be honest about it, like normal people?" Selena frowned. There was nothing wrong with caring about someone. It didn't feel right to hide it.

"Boys are dumb," joked Taylor. "It's friendship that really counts."

It was true. Nick and Selena soon broke up – and so did Taylor and Joe. But in Taylor Swift, Selena had found someone who truly understood her. She knew they would be friends for life.

Luckily, though, there wasn't much time for Selena to stress about boys. Her profile was growing rapidly, and there was an exciting new addition to her CV: animated movies. Selena's warm, rich voice and perfect comic timing meant she was in high demand.

First she provided the voice for Princess Selenia in *Arthur and the Revenge of Maltazard*, then for Mavis in *Hotel Transylvania* (one of Selena's favourite projects!). In *Horton Hears a Who!* Selena voiced *all* of the Mayor of Whoville's 96 daughters. Voice work was a strange experience, so different from being on a TV set. The stars all recorded their parts separately. Selena didn't meet Steve Carrell, who played her on-screen father, the Mayor – or Jim Carrey, who played Horton. Maybe one day!

And it wasn't just Selena's acting career that was taking off. Selena had always loved singing. She had known since she was seven that one day she wanted to become a singer – and now Disney had given her an amazing opportunity. They wanted to sign her to their Hollywood Records label.

The news arrived on Selena's sixteenth birthday. It was a dream come true! But she had a condition: she wanted to sing with a band. She didn't want to be a solo artist. Not yet, anyway.

Disney agreed. Selena's musical journey had begun.

CHAPTER 8

THE SCENE

Every band needs talented musicians – and Selena and her team set out to find them. Selena wanted to be involved at every stage. She wanted her band to be the best it could possibly be!

Finally, after weeks of auditions, they picked four brilliant musicians: Ethan on lead guitar and backing vocals, Joey on bass guitar, Greg on drums and Nick on keyboard. They decided on a band name too: Selena Gomez and the Scene.

Selena loved spending time with the guys – their knowledge of music was mind-blowing. *Cadence? Bridge? Home key? Riff? Instrumental tag? Elision?* Once the boys started talking about music and songwriting, Selena could hardly keep up!

"How do you know all this stuff?!" Selena asked in awe. She had worked with a producer to record the *Wizards* theme tune, but Ethan and the others knew so much technical detail.

"I've been playing ever since I was able to hold a guitar," said Ethan, and the others nodded.

"Same," they agreed.

"It's like you and acting," added Joey. "You do it all the time, so the technical stuff is second nature."

Selena knew she had a lot to learn, but she had very good teachers. Ethan and the rest of the band taught her how to play the guitar and drums. She was also taking vocal lessons to improve her voice.

"I mess up. A lot. Nobody's perfect," Selena told fans, on her vlog. But she like to be pushed outside her comfort zone – it was fun to be learning new things. Eventually, practice would make perfect.

In addition to her fellow band members, Selena was working with some of the best music producers in America, including Ted Bruner, Tim James and Antonina Armato – a production duo also known as Rock Mafia – and the drummer Gina Schock. It was important to find just the right sound for the band's debut album.

"Whose music do you like?" asked Ted.

Selena didn't hesitate. She named her favourite bands. "Paramore. Forever the Sickest Kids. Britney."

"And what do you want to say?" asked Gina.

That was harder. Selena thought about the songs she loved best. What were their themes? Love, fame, being yourself... She wanted to sing about her experience. She wanted to show fans who she was.

Together, Selena and her producers listened to hundreds of songs. These were sent to them by songwriters all over the world, all of them eager to have their work performed by Selena and her band. There were good songs, great songs – and some awful songs too!

"Listen to this," Selena laughed. "It's about a swimming lesson!"

"And this guy has rhymed 'laugh' and 'sloth'!" Gina added. "Seriously?!"

"A song about a sloth? We *have* to use that one!" Selena giggled. Some of these songs were hilarious – she couldn't imagine who would ever record them. But slowly, song by song, the album was taking shape.

Many of the best songs were written by her

producers. Ted, Tim and Antonina, and Gina were all talented songwriters. But the song closest to Selena's heart was the one she had written herself: 'I Won't Apologize'. Her message? Never change who you are to please other people.

Finally, after months of rehearsals, and hours spent writing and rewriting songs, Selena Gomez and The Scene were ready for their first studio session. Selena could hardly contain her excitement as she arrived with the band at the studio. Recording an album! For the very first time!

She looked round at the people who had made it possible – her band, her amazing producers, her brilliant mum Mandy – and realised how lucky she was. It would be her name in big letters on the album cover, but this was one epic team effort.

For the lead single, Selena and Ted had chosen a song called 'Falling Down', written by Gina, Ted and another producer, Trey Vittetoe. The theme was life in Hollywood. Selena liked how the song made fun of fame. She hated how shallow and fake Hollywood life could be sometimes.

"Let's record 'Falling Down' first," said Ted. "Selena, are you ready?"

He didn't need to ask. Before he had finished speaking, Selena was in the vocal booth, headphones on. "Let's go!"

Ted gave her a cue. The red recording light flashed and Selena began to sing.

The vocal lessons were paying off. Selena's voice had always been strong, but her tone was getting better and better. It was warm, rich, expressive.

"That was great, Selena. Really great," said Ted when she had finished. "Can you try it again, and give it more *bite*?"

"Bite? You mean, sound angry?" asked Selena.

"Hmm, sort of. Mocking, I guess. You're mocking the idea of celebrity."

"OK, got it." Selena was an actress. Creating the right emotion was what she did best. She focused on her character and sang the song again, sinking her teeth into the lyrics. Ted was right: bite was exactly what the song needed!

Ted gave her a thumbs up through the glass panel that separated the vocal booth from the desk where he was controlling the sound. "Perfect! Now, I've got an idea..."

Ted played Selena's words back to her. They sounded just as she had recorded them. Selena couldn't help wincing – hearing her own voice on record without a backing track was embarrassing somehow. Especially in a room full of people!

"Now see what you think of this," Ted said.

He played the recording again. But this time it was completely different. It still sounded like her, but...

"It's way more sassy!" said Selena. "Wow! How did you do that?"

Ted had used a synthesiser to make Selena's voice sound more electronic. The sound fitted the words of the song perfectly.

Next Ethan, Joey, Greg and Nick recorded their parts.

"Really go for it, guys," Ted told them. "Drums and guitars especially. Make them sound as aggressive as you can."

On drums and lead guitar, Greg and Ethan channelled their inner rock star. Back on the other side of the glass, Selena whooped. "That was amazing. You guys *rock*!"

Over the next few months, there were 12 more songs to record, and the recording studio began to feel like a second home to Selena, Ethan and the rest of the band. Selena's technical skills were improving with every session, and so was her knowledge of the recording process. She couldn't believe how much she had learned.

Along with her producers and the record label, Selena chose *Kiss & Tell* as the name of the album. The next step? Coming up with a cover look.

Selena had an idea: a simple close-up of a face, and the lips would have a jewelled heart on top of them. The jewels represented fame, a major theme of the album. Selena was delighted when the art director said yes! The face would be Selena's, of course. By now she was used to seeing herself on posters and screens and in magazines – but seeing her face on the front of her first album cover was a dream come true!

CHAPTER 9

RED CARPET

Kiss & Tell was released on 29 September, 2009, and that night Selena and her band gave their first ever televised performance, on *Dancing with the Stars*. The show had many millions of viewers all across America. The pressure was on!

They chose to sing 'Falling Down'. While Ethan and the boys dressed casually in jeans and T-shirts, Selena went with a more glamorous vibe: a gold sequinned playsuit and long, sparkling earrings. It was hard not to be distracted by the professional dancers, Derek and Karina, as they delivered a stunning routine on the dance floor in front of her, but Selena kept her focus. She strode confidently across the floor and looked to the camera every time it panned in on her face. Her acting skills were coming in useful.

There was a thunder of applause as Selena reached the end of the song and Derek and Katrina struck their final poses. She clapped the dancers and they returned her applause. Another amazing team effort!

In the months that followed, Selena and the boys worked hard, taking every opportunity to promote the album on TV, radio and online. In December, they performed 'Naturally', written by Tim and Antonina, on *The Ellen DeGeneres Show*. Just two months later, in February, they performed with Justin Bieber at PopCon. Selena Gomez and the Scene also embarked on their first tour: 18 shows across America and one in London.

And the result of their hard work? *Kiss & Tell* went to number 9 in the US charts.

Selena was over the moon. Her first album, a hit! It hardly seemed real.

Selena felt like she was living two different lives. As a singer, she was spending more and more time in the recording studio and doing gigs with The Scene. When she wasn't singing, she was back on the set of *Wizards* with a magic wand in her hand. She was also filming her first movie as the lead: *Another Cinderella Story*. Singer? Actress? TV? Film? Selena sometimes found it hard to remember who she was supposed to be from one day to the next!

In September, 2009, there was exciting news for the cast of *Wizards*. The first series of the show had been nominated for Outstanding Children's Program at the 61st Emmy Awards, the most prestigious TV award in America. Up against them? *Hannah Montana* and *iCarly*. Selena loved both shows. She had been friends with Miley Cyrus since her guest appearance on *Hannah Montana* the previous year. Could they really win against competition like this?!

The ceremony was to be held at the Nokia Theater in Los Angeles, one of the largest theatres in the US. Selena had walked the red carpet a couple of times before at film premières and music awards – but nothing had been as big as this. All the Hollywood A-list would be at the Emmys, posing for the cameras one after the other, the women in long, glamorous gowns and the men in tuxedos.

"What am I going to wear?" Selena asked Mandy. "I'll need a ballgown, won't I?"

Selena looked at hundreds of dresses in every colour and style. Should she pick something classic? Satin? Silk? Black, maybe? Or something more fun? Sequins? Layers? Something colourful? Her outfit had to look good from every angle, in every light. It had to be fancy... but not over the top. She didn't want to be the actress whose fashion choice was ridiculed online and in the papers the next day!

Eventually Selena chose a pearl-grey dress made of a beautiful floaty chiffon, with sparkly drop earrings that matched her jewelled bodice. It was chic... but with sparkle. Perfect!

On the afternoon of the ceremony, the sun was beating down fiercely on LA. Photographers shouted Selena's name, trying to attract her attention as she stood with her co-stars.

"Selena! This way!"

"Selena, over here!"

Selena smiled and waved. How hot it was! Her

jewelled bodice felt tight in the heat. But at least she wasn't wearing a tux, like David and Jake!

Selena was relieved when the celebrities made their way into the cool of the theatre. She sat with her on-screen family as they watched category after category being announced, along with short clips from each show.

Mad Men won Best Drama.

30 Rock won Best Comedy.

The Daily Show won Best Variety Show.

There were awards for actors, supporting actors, directors, producers, writers, composers, costume designers, make-up artists, special effects... The list went on and on.

Finally it was time. The nominations for Outstanding Children's Program were announced. Selena squeezed the hands of David and Jake on either side of her. Who would it be? She hardly dared take a breath.

'And the winner is... Wizards of Waverly Place!'

Suddenly Selena felt dizzy with excitement. Without knowing how she got there, she was onstage alongside David, Jake and the rest of the cast and crew... with a heavy, golden Emmy award in her hand! It was an incredible feeling. The show was such fun to make. She was bursting with pride for everyone who had created and supported the show – and, most of all, for the fans!

2009 was shaping up to be a huge year for Selena. Both as a singer and an actress, her career was taking flight... big time.

She was an Emmy winner. She had released a hit album with The Scene. She was also the star of not one, but two new movies.

First there was *Wizards of Waverly Place: The Movie*. Selena travelled with the rest of the cast to Puerto Rico for filming. Being away from home with David, Jake and the rest of her *Wizards* co-stars was like being on a massive family holiday!

Then there was *Princess Protection Program*, also filmed in Puerto Rico. Selena's co-star? None other than Demi Lovato. Finally the best friends were back together, playing... best friends!

Like Selena, Demi was also pursuing a pop career alongside her acting. Her first album, *Don't*

Forget, had come out a year before Selena's. The two girls had always dreamed of recording a duet together and, finally, *Princess Protection Program* gave them the opportunity. Their song 'One and the Same' featured on the movie soundtrack.

Filming with Demi was so much fun. It was like old times – minus the big purple dinosaur! They shared a hotel, ordered room service together, went out dancing in the evenings and talked late into the night. They knew all each other's secrets; it felt like having a sister.

But eventually the filming came to an end. Demi had to return to LA to work on her new album. Selena was recording a second album with The Scene and was about to start filming the next season of *Wizards of Waverly Place*.

"We'll see each other back in LA," said Selena, hugging her friend goodbye. Demi's limo was waiting outside the hotel to take her to the airport.

"I'll miss you," said Demi. "Call me every day, you promise?"

"I promise!"

CHAPTER 10

GOODWILL IN GHANA

Selena stepped out of her car into the blazing heat of central Ghana.

She was with Mandy and Brian. They had come to visit some of the poorest villages in the country, where the charity UNICEF was working to help improve life for children. With a lack of clean water, food, medicine and education, these were some of the most difficult conditions in the world to grow up in. All across the country, children were dying of diseases that were easily prevented elsewhere in the world.

A few months ago, Selena had been appointed a UNICEF Goodwill Ambassador. At just 17, she was the youngest in the history of the organisation, following in the footsteps of David Beckham, Shakira, Robbie Williams, Whoopi Goldberg and many other famous names.

Selena hadn't hesitated to say yes when UNICEF approached her. Being famous had so many privileges – lavish parties, luxury hotels, limos, beautiful clothing... The list went on and on. But this new role was a true privilege – being able to use her voice to help people who didn't have one. Selena wanted to show her fans what life was like for children in parts of the world they might not have even heard of previously.

She looked around now with wide eyes. Since flying into Ghana yesterday, Selena had spent all her time in the capital, Accra. The centre of the city had soaring skyscrapers, brightly lit shopping centres, restaurants... It was modern and comfortable. The countryside was very different.

The village she had just arrived in had only a hundred or so residents, who were living in simple huts made of red clay. Water was pumped from a well – the huts had no running water of their own, which meant no toilets either. Children ran between the huts, playing with toys they made themselves out of scraps of plastic, string and other rubbish.

Selena had been told what to expect, but seeing the poverty for real was still shocking.

A smiling young woman was waiting to greet them.

"Welcome!" she said, shaking Selena's hand.

A small group of children clustered behind the woman, with more running to join them. They stared shyly at Selena and her family.

"Come and say hello!" the woman told them.

Selena smiled encouragingly.

"My name's Selena. What are your names?"

One by one, they told her.

Selena was relieved that they could understand each other. English was the official language of Ghana – but she knew that not everyone in the country spoke it. There were over 250 other languages and dialects spoken here!

One of the older girls stepped forward and tugged at Selena's hand.

"My baby brother is over there," she said,

pointing. "Do you want to see him?"

"Yes, please!" Selena smiled. She loved babies. She allowed the girl to lead her to a small hut where a young woman, the girl's mother, stood cradling a tiny infant. The baby was beautiful. His mother – and his big sister – were clearly so proud of him.

"He's eight weeks old," the woman told her.

"Just eight weeks? Wow!" exclaimed Selena. "May I cuddle him?"

"Of course!" The woman placed her sleeping child gently into Selena's arms. "You're lucky that he's quiet. When he cries... oof!" She rolled her eyes.

But Selena's young entourage was getting restless. Small hands tugged at her T-shirt and questions flew at her from all sides.

"Where are you from?"

"Do you like Ghana?"

"Come and see our teacher..."

"...our school..."

"...our library..."

Selena laughed. "Shhhh! You'll wake the baby!"

Handing the sleeping child back to his mother,

Selena followed the children as they ran from hut to hut, calling out to relatives and friends. Everywhere they went, the villagers were busy. Men and women were harvesting crops in the fields nearby. Women were sewing and cooking. Inside a couple of the huts, the sick – including children – were being cared for by relatives.

Selena knew how little money they had. "Is there a doctor?" she asked her guide. "Do people have the medicines they need?"

The guide's answer was honest. "No. Some of those sick children will die if they don't get treatment soon." She explained that the nearest doctor lived an hour away. Medicines were so expensive that few of the villagers could afford them.

It was hard to hear. As a child, Selena and her family had known difficult times – but nothing like this. She had always had food to eat. When she was sick, her parents had always been able to give her medicine. And, like most children from developed countries, she had been vaccinated against the worst childhood diseases.

Here, children couldn't count on any of that.

She hoped that her work with UNICEF would help. The charity needed money. They needed people all across the world to be aware of how their work was directly saving children's lives.

"Over here!" Selena's noisy entourage had moved on to a long, low building. Its roof was thatched with dried palm leaves, like the huts the villagers lived in. There were no windows. Instead, the sides of the building were open to the wind.

"This is our school!"

The school was a single, large room. "Where do all the different classes sit?" Selena asked.

"It's one big class," one of the older children told her. "Sometimes it's hard to study. The teacher hasn't got much time – he has so many little kids to look after."

At that moment, the teacher himself appeared. The children gathered around, telling him their news and asking him questions. Selena could see how much they liked him.

The teacher smiled and shook Selena's hand.

"Not every child can come to school," he explained. "These children are the lucky ones.

Many have to start work from a very young age – or stay at home to look after someone who's ill."

Selena thought about how much she had hated going to school. She had struggled in class and had always felt stupid. But she knew now how lucky she had been. She had taken school for granted. These children wanted an education so badly and many of them might never receive it.

Today was a Saturday so there were no classes, but...

"We've been practising a song!" The children couldn't contain their excitement any longer. "Can we sing it now?"

Selena laughed. She looked at the teacher, who nodded.

In an instant, the gaggle of noisy schoolchildren transformed themselves into a well-choreographed choir. With the smallest children standing in front of the older ones, they performed a routine of dance moves to the music, a traditional song from the village, while the teacher beat time on a drum.

The harmonies were impressive – some of these kids really could sing!

A crowd gathered to watch, and soon everyone was dancing. An elderly woman took Selena's hands and swayed with her in time to the music. "Not like that... like this!" she told her.

"I've got a lot to learn, haven't I?" Selena laughed.

It had been an incredible, life-changing day. Would her visit make a difference? Selena knew she must do everything in her power to make it count.

CHAPTER 11

FROM HOLLYWOOD TO HUNGARY

Back in Hollywood, Selena was determined to do all she could to support UNICEF and the amazing work it was doing in Africa and across the world. So in October 2010, for the second year running, she took up the role as spokesperson for the Trick-or-Treat fundraising campaign. The year before, she had helped raise $700,000. This year was the sixtieth anniversary of the campaign, and Selena was aiming high... $1 million!

"We can do it!" she told her fans. "This is your opportunity. Join me – get involved!"

Selena had lots of ideas. She designed a special Trick-or-Treat T-shirt. It was selling well and raising lots of money. She had also donated items to a charity auction. She was doing interview after interview – and her social media was buzzing. It felt so good to be helping.

And there was more...

"Selena Gomez and The Scene is giving a benefit concert," Selena announced. "On 26th October, here in LA. All the proceeds will go to UNICEF."

The concert was one of Selena's favourites so far. The vibe was relaxed, like a festival. Selena and her band had just released their second album, *A Year Without Rain*, and their fans were excited to hear a mix of old and new music – 'I Won't Apologize', 'Naturally', 'Ghost of You', 'Intuition' – along with covers of some of Selena's favourite artists – Pixie Lott's 'Mama Do', Cheryl Cole's 'Parachute'...

In the studio, the band's music had a fast, electro sound. But here on a small stage, it was fun to perform the songs with just a mic and acoustic instruments. It showed what great musicians her band members were!

But the biggest applause was for Selena's duet with a young fan who had been chosen from the audience to perform 'A Year Without Rain' onstage with her idol. Selena's small co-star was note-perfect... and the crowd went wild!

Selena and her band closed the show with a cover of the classic song 'Magic' with the audience singing along. It was the perfect end to her first acoustic show.

"We love you, Selena!" shouted the audience. Selena felt warm and fuzzy inside. And the best thing? It was all in aid of an amazing cause.

"You being here is helping kids across the world who are much less fortunate than we are," she told her fans. "It means the world to me. I love you guys so much!"

Selena had aimed to raise $1 million. It turned out, with her support, the UNICEF Trick-or-Treat campaign raised $4 million! Selena's posts about the campaign on social media received nearly one billion hits.

It was more than Selena could have dreamed of – and reminded her of something she already knew: her fans were amazing.

When Selena wasn't in the studio writing and recording new music, or on set filming Wizards, she was busy learning new film scripts. In 2010, she had two more movies lined up: *Ramona and Beezus* and *Monte Carlo*. She also had to study, working with a tutor to prepare for her school exams. Selena hadn't attended regular school for many years; her filming and music schedule was too busy. But she knew how important it was to get an education. Her trip to Ghana had shown her that, in the most powerful way possible.

Selena was excited about her upcoming movies. *Ramona and Beezus* was based on a series of children's books about a mischievous little girl, Ramona, and her big sister. She remembered the books from her childhood – they were classics! She couldn't wait to bring Beezus to life on-screen.

Monte Carlo could not be more different. Selena was playing a British girl mistaken for an heiress. She had to learn a British accent, which wasn't easy...

Luckily her *Wizards* co-star, Gregg Sulkin – who played Alex's boyfriend, Mason Greyback – was British.

"You have to help me, Gregg!" Selena begged. "And don't laugh!"

"I'll try not to," Gregg smiled. "Let's hear what you've got."

"I – like – to – take – tea – with – the – Queen," said Selena slowly, in her best British accent.

"Er, needs a bit of work!" said Gregg. "Try it again?"

"I – like – to – take... *I – like – to*... Oh, I can't do this, Gregg!" Selena dissolved into giggles... causing Gregg to snort with laughter.

"You *can* do it," Gregg told her. "But we don't all talk like the royal family, you know! Listen to me..."

The filming of *Monte Carlo* took place not in Monte Carlo itself, but in Budapest, Hungary. Selena was enchanted by the city: it was like the setting of a fairy tale, come to life.

Her favourite time to see the sights was at night. The magnificent parliament building on the edge of the River Danube was lit up in gold, its reflection shimmering magically in the water. The huge Chain Bridge sparkled with hundreds of lights, and Buda Castle, towering above the city, was a breathtaking sight. Selena's phone quickly filled with photos. Everything was so old and interesting – the narrow cobbled streets, the tall, colourful houses, the ornate streetlamps... She also loved the food: spicy goulash and her favourite – pickles!

But Selena's most memorable scene of the movie wasn't filmed in the beautiful city streets. It was a graduation scene in which Selena's character, Grace, and her best friends received their high-school diplomas.

Selena had finished her real-life exams only a few weeks before. Being homeschooled, she hadn't had a graduation ceremony, so acting it on-screen was the closest she was going to get.

"I graduated from high school and got my diploma," she wrote on her Facebook page, posting a picture of her wearing her costume of gown and mortar board.

Hollywood life, it was weird sometimes.

OK, make that all of the time...

CHAPTER 12

LOVE YOU LIKE A LOVE SONG

Back in LA, Selena and her band were riding high from the success of their first two albums. They had a strong fan base, and it was growing with every performance.

They went on a second tour, including performances with some of the most famous singers in the world: Katy Perry, Bruno Mars and Enrique Iglesias. Selena knew how lucky they were. Some artists struggle for years to find success. But her label, Hollywood Records, had been supporting her band every step of the way.

Now The Scene were back in the studio, recording a third album: *When the Sun Goes Down*.

The bestselling track on Selena's first album

had been 'Naturally', written by Antonina and Tim. Now Antonina and Tim had a new idea, a song they'd written with songwriter Adam Schmalholz. They played it to Selena at their studio in Santa Monica.

Selena's face gave little away as she concentrated on the lyrics and the melody. But the song had barely begun when Tim and Antonina saw her foot begin to tap. Then her fingers started to beat time. By the end of the track, she was grinning. "That was incredible! What's it called?"

"'Love You Like a Love Song'," Antonina told her.

"We think it's perfect for you," Tim added.

Selena nodded. She did too. "Can I hear it again?"

This song was just so catchy! Already it was stuck in her head. There was no doubt in Selena's mind. This was *her* song.

"I love it!" she told Tim and Antonina. "And I'd love to record it!"

By the time they got into the studio with the band and began to lay down the track, everyone had the same feeling: this was going to be Selena's biggest hit yet. The song was fast; it was fun. Antonina and Tim suggested a strong, pulsing beat. "It's 'Eurodisco'," they told Selena, who loved the dance vibe.

The tune was so addictive that Selena found herself humming it as soon as she woke up in the morning. She couldn't help it!

It was a special song, and Selena knew it needed an amazing video to go with it. The lyrics were about falling in love and what a crazy feeling it was – maybe the video should be a bit crazy too. So Selena hired directors Geremy Jasper and Georgie Greville. Their videos were often surreal, funny and thought-provoking.

The result did not disappoint.

Selena tried to describe it to Mandy.

"It's set in a Japanese karaoke bar and I'm singing along to my own song. Then I appear on the TV – you can see me on a beach with a hippie-looking guy. Then I'm lying on a piano floating in the clouds, with a pianist who's dressed like Mozart – it's all super weird. Next I'm driving in a car, in space—"

"Stop! Stop!" said Mandy. "It's too crazy! I'm going to have to watch it..."

Selena laughed. "I haven't got to the really weird bit yet."

Her favourite scene was the one where she was standing in a purple field. Ethan and the boys were dressed as a mariachi band, and Selena was hitting a huge, heart-shaped piñata with a pink lightsabre.

Yes, this video was possibly the craziest thing she'd ever done!

Her fans loved it – and they loved the song. Released in June 2011, 'Love You Like a Love Song' was Selena's biggest hit so far. When the band performed it live, the reaction was mind-blowing. By the end of the month, it had sold over two million copies.

"Two million people have bought our record, guys!" Selena squealed.

And soon there was another cause for celebration: they had won the Teen Choice Awards "Best Love Song" category. A star-studded audience watched as Selena Gomez and the Scene performed live and collected their first ever music award.

In the front row, Taylor Swift was cheering and clapping her friend.

And beside her?

Megastar singer Justin Bieber.

CHAPTER 13

JELENA

Selena was sprawled on the sofa at Taylor Swift's beautiful LA apartment. Taylor was sat cross-legged next to her. On the table in front of them was a huge vase of sweet-smelling flowers, a stack of magazines... and a plate full of chocolate muffins. Taylor loved to bake.

Selena reached for a muffin. "These are *amazing*," she said, taking a bite. "Literally the best muffins I've ever tasted."

"Don't change the subject!" Taylor scolded her friend. "You and Justin... what's going on?"

"Well..." A smile spread across Selena's face. "We're kind of an item!"

"I knew it!" Taylor squeaked. "And, by the look on your face, you really like him?"

Selena nodded, her grin growing bigger. "Aw, Taylor, he's amazing. He's cute – obviously. He's funny. He's smart. I've never clicked with anyone like this before. We just have the best time together!"

Taylor pulled Selena into a hug and ruffled her friend's hair affectionately.

"You know you're not going to be able to hide this for ever, don't you?"

Selena grimaced comically and Taylor let out a snort of laughter.

Justin Bieber, the sixteen-year-old Canadian singer, was one of the biggest pop stars in the world. He had hundreds of millions of fans. They both knew how passionate Justin's fans were. The Beliebers weren't going to be happy to find out that their idol was in a relationship...

"There are already rumours on social media," Taylor added. "Maybe you should make it official, get it over with?"

"We're not ready," Selena said. Becoming an official couple was such a big step – even without the whole world watching! "I mean, who knows what's going to happen," she added. "I'm so young.

He's even younger!" Selena was only eighteen, two years older than Justin.

When she had dated Nick Jonas, Selena had seen how hard it was to be in a relationship with another celebrity. And Nick was nowhere near as famous as Justin – no one was! She didn't want to share their relationship with anyone right now, especially not the paparazzi.

"Plus, if we're official, you'll kick me out of the Lonely Girls Club!" said Selena, making puppy-dog eyes at her friend.

The "Lonely Girls Club" was made up of Taylor, Selena and four other single friends. They met regularly at Taylor's apartment to chat and eat Taylor's famous cakes.

"Never!" Taylor smiled. "The Lonely Girls Club has always got a place for you, Selena Gomez."

As the weeks went by, the rumours about Justin and Selena got stronger and stronger. On social media, someone invented a hashtag: *#Jelena*. Paparazzi stalked Justin and Selena wherever they went. They had to be careful not to hold hands, kiss, or even hug. The smallest display of affection would be all over the media within hours. It was so hard!

Finally, on holiday together in St Lucia in January 2011, Selena and Justin let their guard down. They were so happy to be together on the beautiful Caribbean island. How could they not kiss on the gorgeous sunlit beach, with the turquoise sea rippling behind them...

Almost instantly, the photos appeared on phones and computer screens across the globe.

Selena and Justin decided that there wasn't much point trying to hide their relationship any longer – so 'Jelena' went public.

The Vanity Fair Oscars party was their first official outing as a couple. Then, in May, they went together to the Billboard Music Awards, where Justin won the award for Best New Artist. He tried to drag Selena up onstage with him to collect his award. She wouldn't let him, though... this was his moment! But from the audience, she clapped harder than anyone. Her talented, big-hearted boyfriend deserved his success.

Many of Justin's fans hated seeing him with

another girl – but Jelena had lots of supporters too. So Justin and Selena decided to enjoy with their status as the newest Hollywood A-list couple.

Brangelina 2.0, joked Justin on Instagram, posting a picture of him and Selena. Who knew what the future held, and in the meantime, why not have fun imagining?

CHAPTER 14

DREAM DATE

Selena and Justin's limo pulled to a stop outside the towering Staples Center in downtown Los Angeles. It was LA's biggest arena, a major music venue and home to legendary basketball team the Los Angeles Lakers.

"We're getting out here," said Justin.

Blue light poured from the huge glass windows and the giant red letters at the top of the building were glowing brightly. The stadium was silent though. No cheering fans. No din from the PA system. There was no one coming in or out.

"Was there a game tonight?" Selena asked. "Because it looks like we've missed it."

It was late. Selena and Justin had spent the

evening at the Nokia Theater nearby, where Demi Lovato had been performing. Her new album, *Unbroken*, was just out and Demi had given a brilliant gig. Selena was so proud of her friend.

In fact, the whole day had been pretty amazing. Selena and Justin had been hanging out together at Paradise Cove in Malibu. Selena loved this beautiful stretch of golden sand, the elegant palm trees and the endless blue sea. Growing up in Grand Prairie, the coast had been over 250 miles away. Her parents had struggled to fill the car with enough gas to get Selena to school and back – let alone take her on trips to the sea. But now the beach was one of Selena's favourite places to be. If only the paparazzi would stay a safe distance away!

Today, as usual, she had seen them lurking – but even that hadn't spoiled her enjoyment. She and Justin had walked hand in hand along the beach in the warm late-September sunshine and eaten lunch at the famous Beach Café. Justin was going away on tour in just a few days' time, and they wanted to spend as much time together as possible.

Yes, today had been perfect. But why had Justin

brought her to an empty stadium?

"You're not going to sing a concert for me, are you?" she joked.

"It's a surprise," he told her. "Wait and see."

Selena squeezed his arm. Justin was often surprising her with romantic gestures. What could it be? Meeting a basketball player, maybe? But the Lakers weren't her team. Being from Texas, she supported the San Antonio Spurs. She'd told Justin that. Had he forgotten?

The limo swept away and Justin hurried Selena across Star Plaza to the VIP entrance. A guard opened the door and ushered them inside.

Another official then appeared.

"My name's Tia," she said, beaming. "Come this way."

Selena looked around in confusion. It was as quiet inside the arena as it had been outside, but the lights were on and the staff were on duty...

"Seriously, Justin, what are we doing here?"

Her boyfriend just smiled mysteriously.

Selena grimaced. "You are so annoying, Justin. You know that?"

There was no time to dawdle. Tia led them rapidly out of the foyer and along a series of corridors. Some were lined with pictures of Lakers players, past and present. Some had pictures of the artists and bands who had performed here. Bruce Springsteen. Tina Turner. Britney Spears. Beyoncé. Rihanna. Taylor Swift. Lady Gaga... The list was endless.

"Can't see you anywhere, baby," Selena said, teasingly.

"I'm probably not big enough... Oh – wait!" Justin spotted his own photo. "Plenty big enough!"

"No one likes a show-off!"

By now it seemed they were in the bowels of the stadium. Tia continued to march in front of them, turning round every now and then to check that the couple were following her. Eventually she pushed through a door signed *Personnel only*.

"I think we're in the players' area," whispered Selena. She saw a sign to the home team's locker room. She wasn't sure why she was keeping her voice down – somehow it felt like they weren't supposed to be here!

Tia abruptly turned a corner. Now the walls and floor were made of concrete. Their footsteps sounded louder than before and the air felt more chilly. Was this the players' entrance? Tia pushed open a double door and Selena and Justin stepped through it. As the doors sprang shut behind them, they were plunged into darkness.

But only for an instant...

With a brief hum and sizzle, a thousand bulbs flashed into life. The gigantic stadium was suddenly illuminated. The basketball court stretched in front of them, vast and gleaming. Row upon row of seats stretched up to the ceiling. The huge screen above the centre of the court shimmered with a rainbow of colours.

And there wasn't a single other person in the arena. Even Tia had magically vanished.

Selena put her hand to her mouth. "You didn't...!"

"My lady..." Justin took her hand and began to lead his girlfriend across the court. It took a second for Selena to spot where he was heading.

"Justin! This is *too* much!"

At the far end of the court was a table, covered

in a white cloth, and two chairs. Selena could see flowers, sparkling silver cutlery and crisp white napkins. Dinner! All of a sudden, she realised how hungry she was.

"This is completely surreal!" said Selena, flinging her arms around her boyfriend. "I love it, thank you!"

Someone, somewhere, was watching their every move, because as soon as they sat down, a waiter appeared, bringing drinks and a starter, followed by steak and chips, served on a silver platter. As romantic gestures went, this was off the charts, even by Justin's standards!

Then, all of a sudden, the lights dimmed and a haunting melody filled the stadium. The massive screen above the centre of the court lit up with sepia images. A huge ship. Waving crowds on board and on the quayside... followed by a shot of the deep blue sea, and... *Titanic!*

It was Selena's favourite movie, and one of the most romantic films ever made. Justin leaned in to kiss her – and this time no one was watching. No paparazzi. No cameras.

In the middle of a 20,000-seater stadium, for once they were completely, perfectly alone.

CHAPTER 15

WORLD TOUR

While, off-screen, Selena was happily in love with a pop megastar, on-screen in *Wizards of Waverly Place*, her character Alex wasn't so lucky. If she didn't win the competition to become the Family Wizard, she would have to say goodbye – for ever – to her boyfriend, Mason Greenback, the werewolf. It would be a howling shame.

The final episode of the final series of *Wizards* aired on 6 January, 2012. With nearly 10 million viewers, it was the most-watched series finale in the history of the Disney Channel. The fans were on the edge of their seats. What would happen to the characters they had come to love? Would Alex win and stay with Mason? Or would her brothers beat her to victory? Anything was possible!

The actors had filmed the final scenes months before. Selena and her fellow cast members had managed to keep the plot a secret ever since – they couldn't even tell their families!

Selena could hardly believe that *Wizards* was coming to an end. It had been such a special experience, working with such talented actors, directors and crew. On the final day of filming, the whole team laughed and cried together. How much they would miss this colourful, friendly world!

Selena, Jake and David were backstage chatting with the production team when the director called them over. The crew had gathered round. "We've got presents for you," said the director, handing each of them a parcel. "Open them!"

Selena pulled the paper from her parcel. Whatever was inside was long and thin. Could it be...?

"My wand!" gasped Selena. "Thank you."

Selena had held this wand so many times that it almost felt like a piece of her. It was the perfect souvenir of a magical time.

"I'm going to frame it," she declared – but not before giving it one final wizard's flourish.

It was sad to say goodbye to *Wizards*, but Selena Gomez – actor, singer, teen idol – was busier than ever. Her fans still knew her best as Alex Russo, but Selena was determined to rebrand herself as a grown-up singer and movie star.

The first step? *Spring Breakers*. It was her first "grown-up" movie and had been so much fun to make, acting alongside rising stars Ashley Benson, Rachel Korine and Vanessa Hudgens. It was also the biggest production Selena had been involved in so far. For weeks, the beach town of St Petersburg, Florida, had been taken over by actors and film crew. Selena and her co-stars had enjoyed acting alongside real college students on their spring break, who provided the crowd scenes.

And then there was Selena's new album, *Stars Dance*. Finally, after three albums with The Scene, Selena had decided to go solo. She would miss her talented band, but this was a new beginning and she was excited. Up till now, music had felt like a sort of 'professional hobby'. She had thought of herself as an actress who liked to sing. But now it was getting serious... Once the album was released, Selena would be going on her first solo tour – a *world* tour!

Her record label believed in her. Her fans believed in her. But Selena herself couldn't help having doubts. Could she pull it off? Could she make it as a "proper" singer?

One very famous pop star seemed to think so...

Selena was onstage with Ashley and Rachel at a press conference to promote *Spring Breakers*. The actors faced a room full of reporters asking questions. Selena had done many press interviews so far in her career. The questions were usually predictable, almost too easy.

But then a voice from the back of the room piped up: "Ladies, did you lip-sync to Britney Spears? You lip-synced, right?"

The scene that the reporter was referring to was set in a bar, where the girls sang their version of Britney's 'Hit Me Baby One More Time'.

Selena bristled with indignation. How dare he!

Lip-syncing was the worst crime a singer could be accused of...

But she chose to laugh instead. "No lip-syncing," she declared. "Do you want the proof?"

She began to sing the opening notes of the song.

Ashley and Rachel looked at each other. Was this really happening? A live Britney Spears karaoke, at a press conference?

A helpful producer projected the lyrics onto the screen behind them. OK, it was happening! A little nervously, Ashley and Rachel joined in.

"No lip-syncing, I think you'll agree!" laughed Selena when they came to the end of the song.

It wasn't long before a video of the impromptu performance was uploaded to Twitter – and Britney saw it. She posted her response: she loved it. The superstar even suggested a duet!

Selena's heart was in her mouth. She had just been tweeted by her idol! She replied straight away: *My life is made!*

Getting praise from her favourite singer felt amazing. It was the confidence boost Selena needed before setting off on her first world tour. Now she knew she could do it. After all, Britney had told her so!

In mid-August, Selena said goodbye to her friends and family and boarded the first of many planes. She was bound for a new city, a new country and the first performance of her *Stars Dance* show. The tour was starting in Canada, before heading to Europe and the Middle East, then back to the US, followed by Asia and Australia. She would be on tour for seven months.

Selena loved performing live. Her audience meant everything to her; the energy and adrenaline she got from them was like nothing else. Seeing how her fans reacted to her songs – it was the best feeling in the world.

She and her team had put together a show that focused on singing and dancing. She didn't want complicated staging. Apart from her backing singers, there was just a screen playing videos. One of them showed Selena opening a gift box containing the famous sparkly microphone that she always used, with her name written on it in crystals. Via a series of shots of flashing cameras and swirling newspaper headlines, she showed her fans how hard it was to live under the constant gaze of the media. Selena had been a celebrity for most of her life – but she was still figuring it out.

Seeing the world was a dream come true for Selena, particularly visiting Europe. Climbing the Eiffel Tower. Staring up at Big Ben. Wandering round the canals of Amsterdam. Plus Stockholm, Vienna, Oslo... She had been nervous about feeling lonely on tour, but many of her friends came out to visit her: Hollywood friends and friends from Texas too. Selena had kept in touch with girls she'd known since third grade.

And when she wasn't performing or sightseeing, Selena spent hours on Skype and ichat, catching up with friends and family back in the US. She spoke to Mandy every day.

"Mom! How are you? How's Gracie?"

Gracie was Selena's new baby sister, born just a few months earlier to Mandy and Brian. Selena adored her tiny half-sister.

"We're all doing well, honey. Gracie's asleep."

Mandy angled her tablet to show the serene face of her sleeping daughter. "Look – how gorgeous is that!"

Selena felt her heart melting in her chest. A wave of homesickness rushed over her. "I wish I could spend more time there with you, Mom," she said.

"I know, honey. But you're on such a big adventure. Where are you today?"

"Milan!" Selena grinned. "It's crazy. Everyone's so stylish. Even the dogs are stylish! And the food is incredible."

"You look tired though, sweetie. Are you getting enough rest?" Mandy noticed how pale Selena looked. There were dark circles round her eyes.

"There's no time, Mom."

It was true. Preparing for a concert took most of the day. Then, in the evening, Selena spent two hours onstage. Her set list had twenty songs on it.

"I'm OK, Mom, honestly."

But Mandy was concerned. Her daughter often pushed herself too hard. She wished she was there to look after her.

"Try to take it easy, Selena," Mandy told her. "Promise me?"

"I promise, Mom. Don't worry."

CHAPTER 16

TIME OUT

But by the end of the year... disaster.

Toyko – cancelled.
Shanghai – cancelled.
Singapore – cancelled.
Perth – cancelled.
Sydney – cancelled.
Melbourne – cancelled.

The list went on and on. All across Asia and Australia, Selena's fans learned with dismay that the concerts they had been looking forward to weren't going to happen. Selena wasn't coming.

Selena wrote an apology on her website.

She hated to let her fans down.

I need to spend some time on myself in order to be the best person I can be, she wrote. I hope you guys know how much each and every one of you mean to me.

Her fans were devastated – and worried. Was Selena ill? What was going on?

The truth was, Selena didn't know. She was exhausted. Not just tired; it was more than that. The life of a singer and actor was always tiring. This was different. Some days, Selena could barely move from her bed.

She saw one doctor, then another, then another. They all did tests, but it was a year before Selena and her family found out the answer...

Selena was suffering from lupus.

In most people's bodies, the immune system works to protect the body and keep it healthy. But lupus causes the immune system to attack the body, rather than protect it. Selena's body was attacking itself from within. Without a healthy immune system, lupus sufferers can get very ill very rapidly – and lupus was making Selena vulnerable to the sorts of infections that most people's bodies can fight easily.

The cure? Selena and her family were shocked to learn that there was none. Selena's consultant advised chemotherapy, a treatment that would make it impossible to perform for several months. Selena agreed to the treatment. But the disease would always be there. Lupus wasn't a condition that would ever go away.

"The most important thing is for you to take it easy," Selena's doctor told her. "You need lots of rest. You're not getting enough."

It was true. But Selena was scared. Her career was so important to her. She didn't want to turn down opportunities. Most of all, she didn't want to disappoint her fans again.

"You're going to have to be tough with yourself," the doctor insisted. "Put it this way – if you get really sick, you won't be able to work at all..."

With the final leg of her tour cancelled, Selena forced herself to relax. She made a decision: from now on, she would take time out whenever she needed it – no matter the circumstances. It was hard not to feel sorry for herself at times; most

21-year-olds didn't have to worry about their health. But she would work with what she had. She would manage her illness and not let it stop her.

Over the weeks and months that followed, Selena got better at dealing with lupus. Taking things easy did not come naturally, but she learned how to recognise when she needed a break. With careful planning, she found it was possible to perform, record, act – and rest.

Finally, she was able to return to the spotlight.

It was April 2013.

Selena was back onstage and feeling great. Tonight she was performing at the MTV Music Awards. She looked out at a star-studded audience, who were about to hear the first ever performance of her new song 'Come and Get It'.

Wow! Was that Channing Tatum in the front row? And Brad Pitt? Selena felt a sudden rush of nerves. What was she doing here, just metres away from Hollywood A-listers? She felt like an imposter!

But as soon as the music began, Selena's adrenaline kicked in. She tossed her hair and flung herself into the dance moves. Here, onstage, was exactly where she was meant to be! Selena had said goodbye once and for all to her old Disney image. Her new look was bold and confident: an artfully tattered red dress, a sparkling red bindi, black eye shadow and golden ballet pumps. Finally she felt like the "proper" singer she had always dreamed of becoming.

She left the stage to thunderous applause. 'Come and Get It' had been a hit!

Back in her dressing room, Selena flung herself into a chair. Finally, a moment to relax!

Or not... A short, sharp knock on the door caused Selena to jump.

"Come in," she called.

The young backstage runner looked excited.

"Brad Pitt wants to meet you!" she announced. "He's waiting downstairs."

Selena's eyes widened. Really?! One of the world's most famous actors wanted to meet her? But... why?

"Shall I show him up?" the runner asked.

"Er – yeah. I guess. Wow!"

"We'll be back in two minutes."

As soon as the door was shut, Selena panicked. This couldn't be happening, could it? Suddenly she didn't feel like a "proper" singer at all. She felt like hiding. She dived under the table, pressed her face into her knees and stayed there for a minute until her heart stopped beating so fast. Deep breaths!

By the time her visitor arrived, Selena was out from under the table. Cool. Calm. Poised.

"Selena! That was an amazing performance." Brad shook her hand, smiling broadly. "Can I take a picture with you? My kids are the biggest fans of your show!"

Wizards of Waverly Place – there was no escaping it. To some fans, including the Pitt family, Selena would always be Alex Russo!

Smiling, Brad pulled his phone from his pocket – and finally Selena's cool facade cracked. She grabbed her own phone. "Can I have a picture too?!" she squeaked. She felt like a little kid again.

Brad Pitt! It didn't get much bigger than this!

CHAPTER 17

THE HEART WANTS WHAT IT WANTS

Selena stood in front of a huge mirror in the middle of a beautiful dressing room. On the table in front of her was a jumble of perfume bottles, make-up, hair spray and several big vases of flowers.

It looked real... but it wasn't. It was the set of Selena's new music video. The song? 'The Heart Wants What It Wants'.

Selena stared into the mirror. For an instant, a doubt came into her head. Did she really want to do this, make her innermost feelings public for the whole world to hear?

The feeling quickly disappeared.

"I'm ready," she told her producers, Tim and Antonina. "I'm just speaking normally, right?"

There was a microphone taped under the table. Antonina reached to switch it on.

"Yes, normal volume," she told her. "The mic will pick up everything, and we'll edit it afterwards."

"I'm not sure what I'm going to say. I might talk nonsense."

"It doesn't matter," said Tim. "Just speak from the heart. Imagine we're not here. No cameras. No mic. You're all alone."

They stepped away, and Selena began to speak. She thought it would be hard, but actually it was easy. In her mind, the production crew faded away. It was just her, talking to herself – and to Justin.

Since their incredible date at the Staples Center, Jelena's relationship had been a rollercoaster: on and off again more times than their fans could keep track of. But this time, Selena felt sure it was over for good. And it hurt so much.

Selena began to speak – and suddenly the words came flooding out. Her fingers gripped the edge of the dressing table, and tears rolled down her cheeks.

Somehow, though, it felt good to speak her heartbreak out loud.

"Wow," said Antonina when Selena stopped speaking. "That was really powerful, really honest. Are you OK?"

Selena nodded. Reliving her break-up with Justin was the hardest thing ever – but it had been good for her. She felt lighter.

And now she had to focus again. "Over to you. Work your magic!" she said. She knew that just a few seconds of the conversation she had just recorded would be used on the final video. "And please don't make me sound too crazy!"

The song itself had been recorded a few months earlier. Selena and her producers agreed: 'The Heart Wants What It Wants' was her best song yet. Selena had co-written it, and she knew the world would guess instantly that it was about Justin. So why not add her own words, spoken from her heart?

Selena wasn't scared of her fans seeing who she was. Be emotionally honest – that was her mantra, how she wanted to live. And she wanted to help her fans to do the same.

Another day, another dressing room... But this time it was real.

Selena was backstage at the American Music Awards. She was about to sing 'The Heart Wants What It Wants' live for the first time. Taylor would be in the audience: her best friend, cheering her on.

"Fifteen minutes, Selena," called the backstage runner.

"Thanks," Selena called back.

She tried to make her voice sound bright, but it came out choked. The dressing room was full of people – stylists, make-up artists... The air was buzzing with chat and laughter. Selena stared at her face in the mirror. She tried to smile, but her eyes stared blankly back at her. Suddenly the din in the room and the brightness of the lights were unbearable.

Without putting on her shoes, Selena ran out of the room and down the corridor. She headed for the toilets – the only place where she knew she could be alone.

Fumbling for the lock, she shut herself in a cubicle. She slumped against the door, then slid slowly to the ground. Selena closed her eyes and sat with her head on her knees.

And sobbed.

The pressure was unbearable.

It wasn't her fans. It was never her fans. Her fans understood. It was everyone else who wanted her to be this, wanted her to be that. Do this, do that. Say this, say that... She tried so hard to please everyone, all the time!

Sitting there on the floor, with tears flowing down her face, Mandy's words floated into Selena's head: she needed to trust herself. She needed to take control!

Slowly Selena stood up. When she emerged from the toilet, she knew what she had to do.

From now on, she didn't care what anyone else thought. The only people who mattered were her friends, her fans – and herself.

"Two minutes!" called the runner.

By the time Selena returned, there was panic in the dressing room. Her team had realised she was gone. But the star was calm. Without hurry, she smoothed her hair, fixed her smudged mascara and headed for the stage.

'Everybody, give it up for Selena Gomez!'

Selena stood in the darkness onstage. Emotions swirled inside her. She longed to open her mouth and sing. It was when she was singing that she felt most in control.

The silence was broken as the opening to 'The Heart Wants What It Wants' filled the room. The audience heard for the first time those fragments of painful conversation about Justin.

Behind Selena, a huge video screen lit up. An image of barbed wire filled the screen, then shattered glass, then red rose petals scattering like drops of blood.

Selena began to sing. Her voice was rich and soft. Her eyes were glistening with tears. She sung with her whole heart and this time nothing else in the world mattered. Not even her audience. She was singing for herself.

Finally the screen showed light breaking through the clouds, and wings spreading open and soaring into the air. Hope had overcome darkness and pain.

Selena bowed her head.

She had never sung like this before.

There was a split second of silence before the cheers erupted. Selena spotted Taylor in the audience. Her friend was crying too!

It was the first time, Selena knew, that she had been truly, utterly, 100% herself.

CHAPTER 18

TAKING CONTROL

"I've got a project for you," said Taylor. "Do you want to do something really different?"

The girls were back in Taylor's apartment. There was cake, of course, and Taylor and Selena were talking about new beginnings.

"A new project? Bring it on!" said Selena.

She was excited to know what her friend had in mind.

"I want to do an epic video for 'Bad Blood'. Something special." 'Bad Blood' was Taylor's new song, featuring Kendrick Lamar. "And I want you to be in it."

Selena smiled. "Cool. I'm up for that!"

"Here's the thing, though. I want you to be

the anti-Selena. I want you to be the badass villain. My nemesis."

Taylor described the plot.

"I'm playing a superhero called Catastrophe and you're my crime-fighting partner. We've just defeated the gang of guys, but then you betray me. You kick me out of a window... Sound good?"

"Sounds cool," said Selena, grinning.

"I'm injured but I meet this group of girls who take care of me – and we plot revenge on you. You've also got a group of girls who you've trained to take me down. I'm thinking this is all set in London, by the way. The end is a huge standoff. We punch each other and there's a huge explosion. What do you think?"

"Wow. I don't know what to say."

"Say yes!" urged Taylor.

"Yes, OK! Yes!"

"There's more..."

"I thought there might be." Selena smiled at how excited her friend was.

By now, Taylor was almost squealing. "Now I've got you on board, I'm going to get lots of others. Serayah, Cara Delevigne, Jessica Alba, Lena Dunham, Cindy Crawford... You all get to choose your own character name!'

It sounded incredible. Everything Taylor did was amazing. Selena knew how lucky she was to have such a smart, kind, inspiring friend in her life. Who needed a boyfriend when you had friends like Taylor!

Selena had decided to take control of her life – and she was doing just that. The first change: her record label. She had been with Hollywood Records since they had first signed her at sixteen. Her new label was Interscope, home to Lady Gaga, Katy Perry, Ellie Goulding, Madonna and many other major artists.

Then there was her management... Selena had been managed by Mandy and Brian ever since she first starred on *Barney*. But it was time to separate family and business. She wanted to be her own person.

Selena would still be working with Mandy. Netflix had bought the rights to produce the TV adaptation of *13 Reasons Why*, taking on Mandy as an executive producer. Selena was now too old to play the lead, so instead she was going to be an executive producer alongside her mum. It was an exciting chance to try something new – her first role on the other side of the camera!

She also moved out of the beautiful Los Angeles home that she shared with Mandy and Brian. Selena wanted to be independent. She moved into a stylish apartment with her friend Francia Raîsa. Francia was also an actress and Selena liked being able to share the fun and stresses of her work with someone who understood. The two girls loved living together.

And the changes seemed to be paying off. Selena was feeling more confident and creative than ever...

CHAPTER 19

MEXICO

A fiery sunset of pink and gold spread across the horizon. Silhouetted palm trees swayed against the sky. In a quiet corner of Puerta Vallarta, tucked away from the nightlife, Selena lay in a hammock, listening to the sounds of the evening.

The gentle lap of the waves. The swish of palm fronds. The high-pitched rattle of the crickets. The occasional thrum of an engine, as a scooter wove its way through the cobbled streets.

This town had so many memories for Selena, good and bad.

There was the amazing New Year's Eve she had spent here with Justin, chilling by the pool under the stars.

There was their break-up here a year later.

There was the holiday just a few months ago, when paparazzi had snapped her in her bikini and the world's media had body-shamed her. The rage she had felt was still fresh... How dare anyone criticise her body!

But right now, as the sky turned from pink to indigo, and the first stars flickered into life, Selena was happy. LA was her home. Texas was her birthplace. But her roots were here in Mexico. Here she felt connected.

"Can you hear that music?" Selena asked, turning to her friends.

The sound of a solo guitar rose above the other noises. A band was playing in the local bar. Music was Selena's favourite thing about Mexico. She loved the traditional rhythms, the energy and passion. Every song told a story: love and heartbreak, courage and adventure.

Selena felt at her most creative while she was here – which is why she had chosen to bring her production team to this villa by the sea. She hoped they would create some amazing songs here, away from the hustle and bustle of LA.

And of course it was fun to hang out too!

With her were her producers, Tim and Antonina, the rapper and producer Hit-Boy, and two songwriters, Justin Tranter and Julia Michaels. Tim and Antonina had brought recording equipment and had turned the smallest bedroom into a mini studio. The whole group could barely fit into the room together, but Selena felt happier here than in the big studio in Los Angeles. Every morning she woke up fizzing with excitement. Amazing things were going to happen, she was sure of it.

"And, hey, it's nice to be here with people I won't have an epic bust-up with," she joked.

The group laughed.

"How is Justin?" asked Tim.

"He's seeing someone."

There was silence for a moment.

"I'll always care about him," Selena told them. "He was my first love. I want him to be happy."

Justin's friendship meant the world to her and she knew that he felt the same. She missed him, and the media were constantly trying to stir up rumours that they were back together. But they were better as friends, she told herself.

"So what do you want the new album to say?" Antonina asked her. She knew Selena would have a vision.

"I want to write about the pressure to be perfect," Selena answered. "It's not just me feeling like that. It's every young person, famous or not."

Her friends nodded. They all knew how hard the constant media attention was for Selena.

Selena continued. "I want to show how I've come through that stuff. I want to say that anger and bitterness isn't the answer. Love and kindness is. And faith. I want to write about all the things that support me."

Selena gazed up at the sky, now velvety black and glittering with thousands of stars. She knew how lucky she was to do this incredible job. It was a privilege to be able to speak out and to know that millions of people would be listening.

"I want these songs to reflect me," she said. "I'm not scared to be myself any more."

Authenticity, faith, love, kindness. The themes hung in the air, while in the distance the guitar continued to play.

"I have an idea," said Selena. She hummed the first few notes of a tune. "I think it might be the start of something..."

By five o'clock in the morning, the song was recorded. Its name? 'Body Heat.'

Clutching mugs of coffee to keep them awake, Selena and her friends huddled over the recording deck in the tiny makeshift studio. They had been up for 17 hours.

"We did it!" said Antonina.

Selena smiled. She was buzzing from coffee and adrenaline. The fragment of melody that she had sung from her hammock a few hours earlier was now a full track, with lyrics and instrumentals. The guitar had found its place at the start of the song. They had added a trumpet, a saxophone and a traditional Mexican horn. The flavour was Mexican, through and through.

Inspiration had struck – and the right people

had been there at just the right time.

"You guys are amazing," said Selena. "Thank you for making this happen!"

From that day on, in Mexico, then back in the studio in LA, the songs kept flowing:

'Hands to Myself'

'Good for You'

'Same Old Love'

'Kill 'Em with Kindness'.

The last one was particularly personal to Selena, inspired by her experience of body-shaming.

"If I can help just one person who is made to feel bad about their body, making this album will be worth it," she told Tim and Antonina one day, back in the Los Angeles studio.

"One person?" Antonina smiled. "You've got over one hundred million followers on Instagram alone. You're going to help a lot more people than that!"

Selena chose the name *Revival* for the album. That's what it felt like. She had learned so much about herself in the last year. She felt like a different person; a new, stronger, better person. And the music? That sounded different too. Tim, Antonina and the rest of the team had worked hard to give Selena a unique new sound.

The result, rich and sultry, was everything Selena had hoped for.

As she waited for the album to drop, she prayed that her fans would feel the same!

CHAPTER 20

REVIVAL

In October 2015, *Revival* was released. The reception was amazing. Fans and critics alike loved Selena's new sound and her thoughtful, passionate lyrics. Selena was elated. She had written and sung from the heart. She was so happy that her fans understood!

Next stop? A tour.

The *Revival* tour had been months in the planning. Between May and December, Selena would be travelling across North America, Asia, Australia and New Zealand, Europe, the Middle East and South America. Her support act was DNCE, Joe Jonas's band.

Joe had been in her life for a long time now.

He had auditioned for the part of Justin, Selena's on-screen brother, in *Wizards of Waverly Place*. Then of course he had dated Taylor – and Demi Lovato. Selena still liked to tease Joe about the disastrous Central Park date with Taylor and his brother Nick.

"You've dated both my best friends," Selena said slyly one day. "Maybe we should..."

Joe looked shocked. "Oh no, no. Way too weird." He shook his head. "No... I... Selena. . ."

"I'm *joking*! Your face!"

Selena knew she would miss Taylor and Demi while she was away. But she and Joe got on well. It would be fun to hang out with him and his band as they explored new cities, stayed in fancy hotels – and worked hard to put on the best show ever.

Revival would be very different from *Stars Dance*, Selena had made sure of that. There would be more spectacle, more energy, more props, more costume changes. Selena knew she could command the stage more powerfully than before. There was a strong Mexican influence, including Day of the Dead masks. Selena also had decided to reveal her talent for playing the piano... live. If her nerves suddenly took hold, it would be a disaster! But it was worth the risk – as usual, Selena wanted to challenge herself.

The tour started on a warm spring evening in Las Vegas. As her chauffeur drove her through the traffic towards the Mandalay Bay Events Center, Selena could see all the glitz and glamour of Vegas: the breathtaking Bellagio fountain, the glittering Eiffel Tower, the Statue of Liberty, the Great Pyramid, the Venetian palace... It was like a world tour in just one limo ride!

Selena's whole body tingled with excitement. Vegas was so special. She couldn't wait to be onstage.

But there were still hours to go till showtime. Selena sat patiently as stylists gave gloss and volume to her long brown hair, and make-up artists carefully enhanced her features with smoky black eyeliner, mascara and a deep, velvety lipstick. Finally, an assistant helped her into her first costume: a sheer, black, sequin-sprinkled bodysuit.

Standing on the stage in the darkness, the audience stretched further than Selena's eyes could see. The only lights in the stadium were the bright dots of phone screens, like a blanket of stars that seemed to go on for miles. But the cheers were electrifying. Her fans! Almost ten thousand of them!

Selena's heart went out to each and every person who had come to support her. She hoped they could feel it!

The high point of the show was the final song: 'Revival'. Sparks burst from the sides of the stage like fireworks, followed by great clouds of smoke, glowing pink and blue under the lights. Beams of pink light shot across the stadium as showers of coloured confetti rained down on the audience. Finally Selena could see the happiness and excitement on the faces of her fans, their arms raised in their air, dancing and swaying to her song.

"Thank you so much, Vegas!" she shouted. Her heart was pounding as she ran offstage. What an incredible opening night it had been.

And now? The same show – 90 more times!

The next day, Selena and her entourage of production crew, singers and dancers were back on the road, with coaches and lorries packed with costumes, props and scenery. They travelled to Fresno, then Sacramento, San Jose and Seattle. Next up was Canada, then back to the US for six weeks, followed by Quebec City. Then they flew long-haul to Indonesia, for the start of the Asian leg of the tour.

In every city, at every venue, audiences went wild as Selena delivered her epic show.

But tiredness was dragging Selena down. She was performing three or four concerts a week. By the time they reached Tokyo, their final Asian destination, Joe was worried.

"Selena! Selena!" It was the third time he had knocked on the door of her hotel room. "The car's here. You wanted to see the sights, right?"

Selena opened the door. She was still in her pyjamas and he could tell she had been crying.

"I've tried calling you," said Joe. "You didn't pick up."

"I'm sorry. I couldn't."

"You're shaking!" Joe took Selena's hand. It was trembling. "Sit down, Selena. Tell me what's going on."

"I think I had a panic attack. I couldn't breathe. I tried to call but I... it... just..." The words wouldn't come. Selena put her hands over her face. Her whole body shook.

"It's OK. It's OK, Selena."

"I can't do it," she whispered.

"The show?"

She nodded. Tears were streaming down her cheeks.

Joe understood. Lupus caused Selena to experience fatigue, anxiety and depression. Tentatively he said, "We can cancel the show, you know. The whole tour if we need to. It wouldn't be the end of the world."

But that only caused Selena to sob louder. She couldn't! She hated to let her fans down.

Joe put his arms around her. "Think about it. I'll support you whatever you decide to do."

The show did go on. The next day, Selena performed at the Tokyo International Forum. Watching her stride confidently across the stage in her sparkling gold bodysuit, no one would have guessed the anxiety she was feeling inside. It was only when she returned to her dressing room and shut the door that, once again, she broke down in sobs.

She didn't know how she could go on.

Finally, in August, Selena made the decision to take some time out. She had performed 55 shows in 100 days. She had pushed herself as far as she could. Any further, and the results could be disastrous.

With sadness and frustration – but knowing she was doing the right thing – Selena cancelled the second half of the tour: Europe, Saudi Arabia and South America. She was particularly sad about Mexico. She hadn't sung there since 2012, on her last tour with The Scene. Guadalajara would have been the final destination for *Revival*. She knew how special it would have been to end the tour in her spiritual home.

So, once again, Selena rested. It was so frustrating, seeing Joe and his band return to the studio in LA and knowing that she couldn't. But her health was getting worse. There was nothing else she could do. And she made a decision. She would donate the proceeds of the *Revival* tour to the Alliance for Lupus Research. Maybe one day there would be a cure for this debilitating illness.

In November 2016, Selena made an exception to her relaxation rule, appearing at the star-studded American Music Awards. She had been nominated for the coveted award for Favourite Pop/Rock Female Artist. It was a prize voted for by the fans. Selena won, beating Rihanna, Adele, Taylor...

And she realised – health issues, a few months out of the spotlight – none of it mattered. Her 125 million fans simply wanted her to be who she was. It was being honest about all that stuff that made her strong – and special.

Standing onstage to accept the award, Selena thought back to her emotional performance at this same event two years ago, singing 'The Heart Wants What It Wants'.

"In 2014," she told her audience, "here on this stage was the first time that I was authentically one hundred per cent honest with all of you."

At that moment, she told them, she had been broken inside. But not any more.

"If you are broken," she continued, "you do not have to stay broken."

The applause was wild. Her friends, her fans – they all knew how hard she had worked to take control of her career, her health, her life... It was truly inspiring to see.

CHAPTER 21

A FOREVER FRIEND

In a separate operating theatres in the Cedars Sinai Hospital, Los Angeles, surgeons in masks and scrubs bent anxiously over the bodies of two young women.

One was Selena Gomez.

The other was Selena's friend and flatmate, Francia Raísa.

Selena was undergoing a kidney transplant operation. A month earlier she had been rushed to the hospital with kidney failure, connected to her ongoing illness, lupus. Francia was her donor. She was giving one of her kidneys to save her friend's life.

The transplant operation should have taken

two hours, but there was a complication: a broken artery. The surgeons would need to remove a vein in Selena's leg and use it to construct a new artery to replace the broken one. Without it, Selena's new kidney wouldn't stay in place – and she might die on the operating table. Up to six hours of further surgery would be needed. The surgeons worked with painstaking care, while elsewhere in the hospital, Mandy waited anxiously for news.

As Francia awoke from her anaesthetic, she expected to see her friend. But where was she? Had something happened to Selena? Mandy explained. Selena wasn't safe yet. They would have to wait and pray.

Francia and Selena had known each for nine years and, as Selena's flatmate, Francia had seen every day how her friend's health was deteriorating. Selena had been tired and weak. On a really bad day, she had barely had the strength to open a bottle of water.

Then, one day, Selena revealed that she had been for some tests.

"My doctors say I need a new kidney," Selena had told her friend. "Without it I'm going to get sicker and sicker. But the waiting list is seven to ten years." There were tears in her eyes.

A new kidney? That was a huge operation, Francia knew. Patients had to wait for the right kidney to be donated. A patient's body would reject a kidney that wasn't a match.

Francia hadn't needed to think.

"I'll get tested," she blurted. "Straight away. If I can give you one of my kidneys, I will!"

Selena protested – it was such a big sacrifice – but Francia was determined. She thought of Selena as a sister. She couldn't bear to see her friend suffering. It was possible to live a completely healthy life with just one kidney.

In a few days the results came back. It was the result Francia had been praying for. She was a match!

A potential organ donor has to undergo dozens of tests before an operation can happen. There were blood tests, a diabetes test, a CT scan, X-rays... Mental and emotional health must also be tested.

Usually the process took months. But Selena's health was in rapid decline – it was an emergency. Francia took all the tests in a single day. The operation date was set.

A few days later, Francia came home to find that Selena had a surprise for her. Her friend handed her a gift, beautifully wrapped in coloured paper and ribbons. Pulling off the paper, Francia found a box, designed to look like a bible, a symbol of their shared faith. Engraved on top was their special friendship motto: *A sister is a forever friend.*

Inside the box was a kidney bean.

Happy and scared at the same time, Francia hadn't known whether to laugh or cry.

Back in the hospital, Mandy and Francia waited. Nurses came and went. Everyone offered smiles of encouragement, but they felt sick with worry. Mandy took anxious calls from the rest of the family: *How was Selena? Why was there no news?*

The hours went past and eventually Selena's operation was complete. The surgeon appeared... beaming. It could mean only one thing. The operation had been a success!

At last, Mandy could breathe again. In a quiet room, she sat by Selena's bedside as she slowly came round from the anaesthetic. Selena was safe! It was the only thing that mattered in the world right now.

Once Selena was able to move and speak, the nurses wheeled her bed so that it was next to Francia's. Selena reached out to squeeze her friend's hand.

"Thank you," she whispered. "You've saved my life."

Their joy and relief at seeing each other safe was indescribable.

Recovery after the operation was hard for the girls. The pain was excruciating and they experienced depression, which the doctors told them was common after a major operation.

Both girls had scars and decided to display them with pride. Selena didn't care what people thought. Her body was a living, changing thing. She accepted that it would never be perfect, and wanted to send a message to her fans – they didn't need to be perfect either.

"Do you ever regret what you've done?" Selena asked her friend one day.

"Never!" Francia smiled. "I'll always be glad I helped you."

Selena believed her. It was such a relief to know that Francia was happy with her decision.

And Francia had a question too. "Does it feel weird having a bit of my body inside you?"

"Very!" laughed Selena. It really did!

After a few months, both girls had recovered and felt full of energy. Francia had won a role in a new show, *Grown-ish*. She was excited to be back on set, doing what she loved.

And Selena? Her next project was the second series of *13 Reasons Why*, working with her mum as an executive producer. She was so proud of the show they were making together!

Selena's passion for change was getting lots of attention too. She was making a difference as a spokesperson, whether she was speaking at

MELANIE HAMM

WE Day, promoting UNICEF, giving benefit concerts or simply encouraging young people to be themselves, to reject hate and embrace kindness. In September, *TIME* magazine had featured her in a piece on female leaders. Alongside her: Ava DuVernay, Hillary Clinton, Ellen DeGeneres and Gabby Douglas. It was amazing to keep company with these inspiring women.

Then, on 30 November, 2017, Selena won one of the biggest accolades of her career so far: Billboard Woman of the Year. Past winners included many of the biggest names in pop: Beyoncé, Taylor Swift, Lady Gaga, Madonna, Katy Perry, Pink... Selena herself had won Billboard's Chart-Topper award in 2015. But... Woman of the Year! This was epic!

The award rewarded 'success as a recording artist, contributions to the business, and leadership'. That night more than ever, Selena was aware of what a huge platform she had. It was a massive responsibility to be able to speak to so many fans across the globe. She wanted to use it right – to try to change the world for the better.

And, of course, Selena knew exactly who she

wanted to dedicate her award to: Francia, the 'forever friend' who had saved her life.

But Selena still wanted to do more. Being a spokesperson was all very well, but was there something more concrete she could do? Something that would help people in a real way, every day?

For a few months, she'd had the glimmer of an idea in her mind. Now it was time to see if she could make it a reality...

CHAPTER 22

A21

"OK, Selena, this is your key card. It gives you access to the main and side entrances. Here's the photocopier code. Your email address and extension number are on the first page of the hand-book. Any IT issues and you'll need to call the helpdesk on this number here. Any questions?"

Wow, there was so much to take in. It was like the first day on the set of a new show. Except this time, the set was weirdly... *real*.

In fact, it was the first day of Selena's internship at A21, a not-for-profit anti-slavery organisation. Like the rest of the interns, she would be working five days a week, doing a range of tasks while learning more about the charity. Selena had never worked in an office before. Her life was usually spent in recording studios, film sets and concert venues. This was all so new!

Oh, except...

A smile flickered across Selena's face as she remembered the office scene in Taylor Swift's 'Bad Blood' video, where she had helped Taylor, aka Catastrophe, fight a gang of criminals before kicking her friend out of the window. She decided to keep that thought to herself!

Selena believed passionately in the aims of A21: to abolish modern slavery across the world. Human-trafficking was happening on every continent. She knew it was happening right here in California. People were being forced to work unpaid in all types of industries, from farms and factories to restaurants and beauty parlours. It was crazy that people weren't talking about it. Why wasn't it front page news every single day?

"Just one question," said Selena eagerly. "What can I do first?"

The strategy of the A21 team was 'Reach. Rescue. Restore'. First of all they wanted to prevent modern slavery by reaching individuals at risk. They also looked for and helped individuals already caught up in slavery. Finally, they provided care and support to former slaves, so they could go on to lead normal lives.

One of Selena's first tasks was to accompany a more experienced colleague to meet rescued slaves. Their stories were heartbreaking. Listening to these men, women, and sometimes children, offering all the care and kindness she could, Selena knew she had made the right decision: this was the real, practical help that she wanted to give to people who needed it.

By the end of the week, Selena already felt part of the team. Her colleagues were truly inspiring. They were so motivated. They had so much knowledge. Was it weird for them, she wondered, having a pop star for a colleague? If it was, they were far too professional to show it. They just treated her like a regular intern. At last, she could be a normal 25-year-old – *without* the world watching!

No one would let her fetch coffee though.

"I thought all interns did that?" Selena laughed.

"You mean I've clocked all the nearest coffee shops for nothing?"

It was 1.30 a.m. on 22 September. Selena couldn't sleep. She roamed around the house, made a drink, had a snack. As she scrolled the notifications on her phone, she had a sudden urge to reach out to her fans. She had taken a step back from social media over the past few months, but out there were millions of fans who loved and supported her – and she wanted them to know that she loved them back.

She flicked to Instagram Live. In a single click, the video camera was filming. Selena Gomez was live online. What did she want to say? She wasn't sure... but she would figure it out as she went along!

"Hello, everybody!" Selena waved at the camera. "I'm doing a live video because I feel like talking to you guys."

This felt good.

"I miss you!" she continued. "I'm here so... ask me any questions. Let's try this."

And they did. Questions came from fans all over the world.

Was a new album coming? "Yes!"

Selena hadn't released an album since *Revival*. She was working on the next one, alongside A21 and her other projects. It had to be just right, something really special. She didn't want to rush it.

A new tour? "Yes!"

The press? Selena frowned.

The media had caused her such stress and anxiety in the last few years.

"Annoying!" That was the word. Then she smiled. "But I've realised that anything I want to say, I can say to you guys directly, right here." Selena liked this new way of connecting!

There were lots of questions about social media. It seemed so crazy to Selena that everyone was obsessed by how many followers she had. "It's just a number," she told her fans. "But it's the same for you guys, I know that." She knew how hard it was for young people growing up with social media, being judged online. The pressure was the same with 100 followers as it was with 100 million.

The questions kept coming.

Was Selena happy? "I am!" Life was good, and she wanted to share it!

Some of the questions were on serious subjects. Fans wanted advice on dealing with depression and panic attacks.

"Get to know yourself," Selena said to her fans. "Figure out why you feel this way."

She had experienced so many of the things her young fans were going through. Anxiety. Depression. Break-ups. Body shaming. Bullying. Living with illness. If she could help her fans on their own journeys, that was an incredible feeling.

And friendship? "My friends are the most amazing people in the whole world," Selena said, smiling. "My best friends have literally saved my life."

An easy question next...

"Taylor Swift? She's awesome! She's like my big sister. I tell her everything."

Selena and her fans talked online for 40 minutes. Talking to her fans directly was like talking to a friend. It felt so good to be open, honest, real. Her fans were what motivated her, always. After all, they were the people who allowed her to do what she loved.

A tiny part of her was nervous about how her management team and the media might react in the morning. But it didn't matter. It was 2.10 a.m. Everyone around her was asleep. Right now, it was just Selena and her fans all around the world...

"I guess I'm going to wrap this up," she told her fans. "But I'm going to do more of this."

Selena had one last thing to say.

"I look crazy. I have this cold sore. And this pimple. But I don't care. *This is how I am*. Goodnight, guys. I love you very much."

CHAPTER 23

HAPPY BIRTHDAY, SELENA

It was 22 July, Selena's birthday. She was 26.

For Selena, birthdays always meant taking time to reflect. So much had happened in the last year... Her internship at A21. Her life-saving kidney transplant. Being named Billboard Woman of the Year. The end of her on–off relationship with Justin Bieber – Justin was engaged now. Winning Favourite Pop/Rock Female Artist at the American Music Awards. *13 Reasons Why* becoming a hit show on Netflix... A rollercoaster year? That was an understatement!

One thing had kept Selena going during the epic highs and lows: friendship. She had Taylor and Francia, of course, and her cousin Priscilla. Then there were Courtney, Ashley, Raquelle, Caroline, Connar, Sam, Anna... Selena had so many people in her life who cared deeply about her.

And her friends were determined to give her the best birthday weekend ever!

Firstly an Imagine Dragons concert – one of Selena's favourite bands. The opening act was Grace VanderWaal, the young singer and ukulele player from Kansas who had found fame on *America's Got Talent*. Simon Cowell had been impressed enough to call her 'the next Taylor Swift'. Grace was a big fan of Selena's – and the feeling was mutual.

When Selena arrived backstage to congratulate Grace...

"Happy birthday to you! Happy birthday to you! Happy birthday, dear Selena, happy birthday to you!"

Grace led the singing, strumming on her ukulele. There were flowers and cupcakes with *Happy Birthday Selena* written in blue icing.

"Yay – a backstage party! This is *sooooo* sweet!" cried Selena, giving the young singer a hug.

"When I heard you were coming, I wanted to do something special," said Grace.

Taylor was three thousand miles away in New York – but she had prepared a cake too, homemade of course. She posted a picture on Instagram: a huge sponge with pink icing, a huge heart in the middle and the words *Gomez or Go Home*.

Selena doubled up laughing. If only her friend were here in California. She missed her so much – and that cake... well, just looking at it was making her drool.

Then... a pool party! Selena and her friends spent the day lounging by the pool at her new house in Newport Beach. Selena had recently moved there from Los Angeles. She felt more relaxed, away from the pressure of LA. Newport's miles of golden sandy beach, epic sunsets and the blue sea stretching to the horizon were Selena's idea of heaven.

But the biggest surprise was yet to come...

"Where are we going?" Selena asked as her friends led her from the villa down to the harbour.

Hundreds of sparkling white boats bobbed on their moorings, while, across the water, the setting sun was surrounded by a halo of fluffy pink clouds.

Selena reached for her phone to take a picture. It was so beautiful.

"Almost there," said Connar. "Now which one? These boats all look the same!"

But suddenly – there it was. Unmistakable! A sleek, white cruiser, decorated in banners and balloons. From the deck, the skipper was waving.

And in the cabin?

Selena squealed with delight. "You guys! This is amazing!"

Her whole family was there: Mandy, Brian, Selena's little half-sister Gracie, her cousin Priscilla. All the people she cared about most in the world, plus...

"Oh my god, I have never seen so much pasta!"

The girls had hired a chef to create Selena's favourite Italian dishes – plus some new ones to surprise her. Ravioli, linguine, tortellini, fettuccine, campanelle... The smells drifting from the small galley kitchen were incredible. It was going to be the world's most delicious party!

The guests were served by waiters in tuxedos, and as they ate, a string quartet played in the background. Then, as the golden sun finally vanished, fairy lights came on, lighting up the cabin. It was magical – the perfect end to a perfect day.

"It's been *the* best birthday," said Selena, hugging her friends tight. "Thank you!"

And Selena's fans, the Selenators, also wanted to be part of the love on her special day: her birthday Instagram post got 10 million likes, and 162,300 comments. It was just a number... but still, it felt good to be connected to these amazing individuals all around the globe.

Back onboard the ship, it was time for Selena's family to go home. It was way past little Gracie's bedtime! As soon as Selena had waved them off, her friends pulled her onto the dancefloor. The DJ was taking requests, and everyone had something cheesy they wanted to hear!

Selena and her friends danced and talked late into the night. She felt blissfully happy, surrounded by the people she cared most about in the world. Would the next year be another rollercoaster? No one had the power to predict the future. But whatever happened, with friends like these, her amazing family and her loyal fans – Selena knew she could handle *anything*.

Turn the page for a sneak preview of another
inspiring *Ultimate Superstars* story...

TAYLOR SWIFT

Available now!

978-178-7-415-201

CHAPTER 1

THE SQUAD

In the middle of Hyde Park, London, a sea of fans stood in the golden summer sunshine watching a huge stage between the trees. Hundreds of colourful homemade signs swayed gently in the breeze. Each one was lovingly decorated with a slogan:

T Swift

Swifty

I Heart Taylor Swift!

Swifties 4Ever.

Some fans had even dressed up as Taylor Swift's famous cats, Olivia and Meredith, the stars of her social media feeds. "We love you, Taylor Swift!" they screamed. "Taylor! Taylor!"

There wasn't long to wait now. The noise of the crowd got steadily louder, excited whoops and cheers filling the air.

Suddenly – dressed in a blue metallic skater skirt, green sequinned jacket and white-rimmed shades – Taylor appeared onstage. Screams rippled through the audience like a Mexican wave. Hyde Park was ready!

As the first notes of 'Welcome to New York' floated across the park, the singer's image appeared on three vast screens. The crowd was on its feet now, holding their signs high, hugging their friends, dancing, and singing along with the familiar lyrics.

Onstage, Taylor smiled at her huge Hyde Park audience. She had travelled the world many times over, but London would always have a special place in her heart. Above her was a perfect summer sky, bright blue and dotted with fluffy clouds. Ancient, green trees towered on either side of her. Just out of sight was historical Kensington Palace. Yes, London was magical.

And today, 28 June, 2015, 65,000 people had turned up to share it with her. This crowd was bigger than it would be in most of the stadiums she had played in. The audience stretched further than Taylor could see.

As she sang – hit after hit from her new album, *1989* – the bright afternoon sunshine faded into twilight. The beautiful park was silhouetted against a dusty golden sunset. Floodlights fired into life, beaming down onto the stage, lighting the trees on either side with an ethereal glow and making the sequins of Taylor's silver dress shimmer. She had already changed costume three times!

Taylor had just sung 'Love Story', supported by her amazing troupe of twelve dancers and four backing singers. Her audience waved their phones, the lights glimmering in the darkness. How romantic it was, thought Taylor. The perfect setting for her most romantic song.

But it was time to switch things up.

"London, England, Hyde Park," announced Taylor, "please welcome to the stage one of your own, Miss Cara Delevingne..."

Onto the stage walked the model Cara Delevingne. She was waving a huge Union Jack.

The crowd went wild. And that wasn't all... Behind Cara came the models Kendall Jenner, Karlie Kloss, Gigi Hadid and Martha Hunt, and the tennis player Serena Williams.

"These are my friends!" said Taylor, grinning.

Together they strode along the catwalk stage, then stood arm in arm to sing 'Style'. Taylor's fans knew how important friendship was to her. These women were more than A-list party pals – they were her Squad. Her mates. Her BFFs. Her besties. They were the people she turned to when she needed advice and support, and to share her joys and sadnesses.

Who else but Taylor Swift would fill a stage with friends?

Taylor's final song was 'Shake It Off', a fan favourite. The video for the song featured some of her own fans dancing alongside professionals. Here, in the middle of the park, the crowd was part of the action too. Taylor danced at the end of a mechanical bridge that stretched into the audience like a crane, hovering just above their heads. The star was almost close enough to touch!

And the Swifties joined in, belting the anthem into the night – 65,000 people singing as one. The stage in front of them was lit like a kaleidoscope of magical, changing colours, while above them the London sky was a clear, deep indigo. It was an evening they knew they would never forget.

And Taylor wouldn't either.